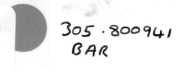

Black youth on the margins

A research review

Ravinder Barn

The **Joseph Rowntree Foundation** has supported this project as part of its programme of research and innovative development projects, which it hopes will be of value to policy makers, practitioners and service users. The facts presented and views expressed in this report are, however, those of the author and not necessarily those of the Foundation.

Published for the Joseph Rowntree Foundation by YPS

ISBN 1 84263 044 X

Cover design by Adkins Design

Prepared and printed by:
York Publishing Services Ltd
64 Hallfield Road
Layerthorpe
York
YO31 7ZQ
Tel: 01904 430033 Fax: 01904 430868 E-mail: orders@yps.ymn.co.uk

CONTENTS

ACKNOWLEDGEMENTS

I would like to thank the Joseph Rowntree Foundation for supporting this work. I am grateful to Charlie Lloyd, Senior Research Fellow at the JRF, for his continual encouragement and helpful comments on an earlier draft of this review.

1 INTRODUCTION

An extensive body of literature into 'race', ethnicity and youth has accumulated over the last few decades. Much of the focus has been on African Caribbean and South Asian young people. Also, the over-emphasis on problematisation has resulted in an imbalance of what we know about minority ethnic[1] young people.

There are three important omissions in the literature. First, mainstream literature has, by and large, excluded minority ethnic young people from study. Consequently, a whole range of diversity is missed and there is a dearth of theoretical and policy-related research addressing the issues and concerns of black and white youth side by side. Second, within the 'race' and ethnicity literature, there has been a lack of effort to bring together the disparate areas of focus to present a coherent picture of the disadvantage and discrimination experienced by minority ethnic young people in Britain. Third, the voice of the minority ethnic young person has been given little recognition.

This review explores the wide range of areas in which minority ethnic young have been found to be disadvantaged. Research evidence suggests that, unless areas of risk and vulnerability are seriously addressed at policy and practice level, minority ethnic young people at the margins of society will become increasingly disaffected and alienated.

This review places a particular focus on:

- homelessness
- under-achievement at school
- school exclusions
- juvenile justice
- 'looked after' young people
- substance misuse
- racial abuse and racial bullying
- racial and cultural identity
- mental health difficulties.

It is hoped that the bringing together of the differing range of areas in one accessible form will act as a useful guide for practitioners, policy makers and researchers.

This review does not claim to be comprehensive. It has not included some areas such as sexuality, teenage pregnancy, physical ill health, and learning and physical disability. Lack of adequate research into these areas is largely responsible for this omission.

The focus of many research studies has been on the adolescent grouping (age 13–19). Some studies into homelessness and employment have included young people between 18 and 24. Consequently, this review reflects the findings as they relate to these groups of young people.

The notion of ethnicity has become increasingly complex and contentious with global movements of people and the development of multi-cultural, multi-racial societies. The social constructs of 'race' and nationality further complicate the picture. Ethnicity is generally perceived to refer to shared cultural, linguistic and religious commonality, whilst 'race' is perceived to denote physical characteristics between people, and nationality and citizenship are intertwined entities. The use of terms such as ethnicity, diversity and cultural minorities in the absence of any reference to race and racism ignores the power relations in society. Differences between people are reduced to their ethnic make up and do little to challenge the power structures.

This review is bound by definitions employed by researchers in their studies, but makes a conscious attempt to contextualise the different minority ethnic groups within the broad framework of multi-racial, and multi-cultural Britain. Due to the paucity of research into small and more recently settled minorities, it has not been possible to focus on groupings such as Kosovans, Albanians, Somalians, Croatians and Bosnians.

Demographic context

Minority ethnic groups, according to the Census in 1991, constituted 5.5 per cent of the total population in Britain. The 1991 Census documents the numbers shown in Table 1.

Table 1 UK population by ethnic group

Ethnic group	Total (in thousands)	%
White	51,874,000	94.5
Indian	840,000	1.5
Pakistani	477,000	0.9
Bangladeshi	163,000	0.3
Chinese	157,000	0.3
Other Asian	198,000	0.4
Black Caribbean	500,000	0.9
Black African	212,000	0.4
Black other	178,000	0.3
Other groups	290,000	0.5
All ethnic groups	54,889,000	100.0

Souce: 1991 Census.

It can be seen in Table 1 that there are wide variations in the representations of different minority ethnic groups. Indians, for example, are the largest minority ethnic grouping followed by black Caribbeans, Pakistanis and others. The Indian group constitutes a range of different religious groups, the majority of whom are Hindu, Sikh or Muslim. The Pakistani and Bangladeshi groups are almost exclusively Muslim. A population breakdown by religious grouping, therefore, could reflect a different picture where perhaps Muslims are the largest group (Modood *et al.*, 1997). The 2001 Census includes a question on religion and should provide a clearer picture of the size of religious groupings.

Official statistics, though useful, need to be treated with caution. For example, the ethnic origin categories employed in the 1991 Census data gathering create much confusion because of their inclusion of 'colour' (white and black) and geographical family origin. It is generally accepted that the term Caribbean refers to people of African ancestry who have migrated to Britain from the Caribbean islands. This term is not normally used to include people of other ethnic groups such as Indian or white from the Caribbean. However, it would be inaccurate to assume that these figures give an exclusive and realistic picture of the British Caribbean population. Interestingly, Modood *et al.* (1997) found that the majority of those of Indian Caribbean origin in their survey described themselves as black Caribbean.

It has also been documented that some Caribbean people defined themselves in historical terms as 'black African', and others (particularly young people) employed a more modern definition of 'black British' and were therefore described as 'black other' (Ballard and Kalra, 1994; Modood *et al.*, 1997). The 'black other' category also includes those of mixed African/Caribbean/ white origin. Such is the nature of ethnic categorisation. The data collated can never claim to be a full representation of a particular ethnic grouping. It is important to be aware of the complex and problematic nature of ethnic categorisation, and the implications of this in ethnic record statistics. It has been argued that, with some exceptions, family origin holds greater significance for individuals than group membership (Modood *et al.*, 1997), and may be a more accurate way of determining the size of particular groups. For example, as mentioned above, the fourth Policy Studies Institute (PSI) survey found that Indian people from the Caribbean perceived their family origin (Caribbean) to be more significant than group membership (Asian) and ascribed a black Caribbean description to themselves (Modood *et al.*, 1997).

Given the social, political and demographic changes over the last ten years, it will be interesting to observe the population patterns in the new Census in 2001. The inclusion of the 'mixed' category and its four sub-categories ('white and black Caribbean', 'white and black African', 'white and Asian', and 'any other mixed background') should also provide a new data set on the growing mixed-ethnicity population.

Black young people

In 1991, black minority ethnic children represented about 9 per cent of the total child population. Overall, there are about a million children from a black minority ethnic background in Britain (nought to 16 years of age). The minority ethnic population in Britain is on average, younger than the white population. Overall, one-third of people from minority ethnic background are under 16 compared with one-fifth of the white population (see Table 2).

It can be seen in Table 2 (see column headed 'All under 16') that the two largest groups of minority ethnic young people are those of Indian and Pakistani background (248,000 and 203,000 respectively). The latter constitute almost 43 per cent of the total Pakistani population in Britain. The Bangladeshi population is also relatively young with children under 16 comprising almost half of

Table 2 Children by ethnic group and age in Britain in 1991

Ethnic group	All under 16 (thousands)	% of ethnic group population
Black Caribbean	109	21.9
Black African	62	29.3
Black other	90	50.6
Indian	248	29.5
Pakistani	203	42.6
Bangladeshi	77	47.7
Chinese	37	23.3
Other Asian	48	24.4
Other	121	41.7
All minority ethnic groups	996	33.0
White	10,027	19.3
All ethnic groups	11,024	20.1

Source: 1991 Census.

this group. Ahmad (1996, 1998) in her study of fertility behaviour has shown the persistence of relatively high levels of fertility amongst women of Pakistani origin living in Britain. She argues that this is probably similar to women of Bangladeshi origin, but is underpinned by a radically different value system to most non-Pakistani women. This is explained in terms of a different notion of the family and its internal dynamics, and as a result of a distinctive set of values and norms surrounding motherhood and wider gender roles. Modood *et al.* (1997) have argued that family size in these communities has enormous implications for family structure and standard of living. The importance of other factors such as poverty, poor housing and ill health are also significant as discussed below.

The Census figures do not as yet collate information about those of mixed racial and ethnic background. However, estimates suggest that there are about 350,000 individuals of mixed ethnicity who make up a significant proportion (11 per cent) of the combined minority ethnic population in Britain. Over 80 per cent of the mixed population are UK-born and over half are under the age of 15 (Haskey, 1997). According to Berrington (1994), more than one in five of all minority ethnic children in Britain under the age of four years is of mixed parentage.

Socio-economic factors

The situation of children and young people is inevitably affected by the socio-economic circumstances of their families. There is a considerable body of evidence which has documented the socio-economic disadvantage and deprivation experienced by black groups in British society as a result of unemployment, low income, poor housing and limited educational opportunity. The pervasive nature of racial discrimination and disadvantage, and in particular institutional racism, has been consistently highlighted by public inquiries and academic research into race relations (Daniel, 1968; Smith, 1977; Scarman, 1982; Brown, 1984; Modood *et al.*, 1997, Macpherson, 1999).

Employment

Post-war migration from the Caribbean and the Indian sub-continent was predominantly driven by economic factors (Sivanandan, 1978). The particular relationship between Britain and its colonies and ex-colonies, built on colonialism and slavery, was an important factor in the migration pull to Britain. Research evidence from this early period of significant migration shows the widespread nature of racial discrimination, and documents that, in spite of their qualifications and experience, Asian and Caribbean people were largely confined to low-paid, manual jobs (Daniel, 1968; Smith, 1977).

Economic theorists have attempted to explain the situation of minority groups in the labour market in various ways. There has been a shift away from perceiving the experiences of black people as a unitary class (Miles, 1982), to recognising ethnic diversity and the different ways in which racial exclusion may affect different groups (Cross, 1989, 1994). Modood (1997, p. 84) argues that the divide in employment and ethnicity is 'not a Black–White divide, but a divide between Whites, Chinese, and African Asians on the one hand, and Bangladeshis and Pakistanis on the other, with Indians and Caribbeans in perhaps an intermediate position.' In addition to the impact of 'race' and racism, it has been suggested that other variables such as gender, religion and culture also influence employment opportunities (Anthias and Yuval-Davis, 1992; Bhavnani, 1994).

Modood *et al.* (1997) found striking differences between different minority ethnic groups in terms of employment patterns. For example, it was found that Caribbean men were twice as likely to be unemployed than their white counterparts (31 per cent), and Bangladeshi and Pakistani rates were even higher (42 and 38 per cent respectively). In terms of female employment, the survey showed that Pakistani and Bangladeshi women were much more likely to be economically inactive than other groups (39 and 40 per cent respectively).

Research evidence since the early 1980s has continued to point to the high levels of unemployment, increasing participation in self-employment and experiences of racial discrimination in employment opportunities (Brown, 1984; Jones, 1993; Wrench and Solomos, 1993). It is evident that unemployment and redundancy among some minority ethnic groups is considerably higher than that of whites (OPCS, 1993). Moreover, a disparate impact on minorities is manifest in the context of poverty (Kaushika and Oppenheim, 1994). Oppenheim and Harker (1996, p. 130) document that minority ethnic people are 'more at risk of unemployment, low pay, poor conditions at work and diminished social security rights'.

The relationship between unemployment, racial discrimination and self-employment has also been highlighted by some researchers (Ward and Jenkins, 1984; Waldinger *et al.*, 1990). Luthra (1997) notes that during 1970–90, a period of increased risk of unemployment, self-employment amongst ethnic minorities increased at a higher rate than amongst whites. Ethnic variations amongst this self-employed grouping have been identified by the recent PSI report (Modood, 1997). It has been documented that the Indians, East African Asians and the Chinese are more likely to be found amongst the self-employed than whites, whilst the Pakistanis are on a par with whites, and the Caribbean and the Bangladeshis are only half as likely as whites to be self-employed. There is also evidence to suggest that, in spite of economic recession, racism and lack of training, Asian business in particular has managed to survive due to familial structures and support, and cultural customer loyalty (Ram, 1992). In the case of big business, financial protection from overseas and international links with the Indian sub-continent have been identified.

Housing

Racial discrimination experienced by black groups in the housing sector has been well documented by research studies highlighting the covert racism of local authority housing policies and allocation procedures, as well as the poor quality of housing given to black tenants compared to white tenants (Daniel, 1968; Brown, 1984; Phillips, 1987; Commission for Racial Equality, 1989/90; Lakey, 1997).

The concentration of black groups in particular geographical areas has been explained in terms of two theoretical perspectives

– 'choice and 'constraint'. 'Choice' theorists have argued that black groups may prefer to reside in areas where there are high numbers of individuals from a similar racial and cultural background as themselves. Such locations have been conceived in terms of communities which serve to provide social support, as well as shared linguistic, cultural and religious traditions (Dahya, 1974; Khan, 1977; Anwar, 1979). 'Constraint' theorists, on the other hand, have argued that black groups have been prevented from moving outside these areas by a range of factors including their economic position, lack of information about housing opportunities elsewhere and discriminatory practices on the part of the white community. Migration settlement patterns of black groups have arguably been affected by economic position and community networks. Moreover, members of black communities also have the added variable around racial harassment and racial discrimination which may act as a significant determinant in 'choice' and/or 'constraint'.

Robinson (1993) shows that minority groups have become more concentrated into urban areas during the last decade. The cities with the largest concentrations are London (1.3 million, or 45 per cent of Britain's black population), Birmingham (207,000) and Manchester (148,000).

The groups which are highly represented in the South East of England include Indian, Caribbean and Bangladeshi (Owen, 1992–95). It is interesting to note that over half (53 per cent) of Bangladeshis reside in Greater London. Nearly half (43 per cent) of the London Bangladeshis are found in the single borough of Tower Hamlets. This means that nearly a quarter (23 per cent) of the total British Bangladeshi population live in a single London borough. The particular needs and concerns of this group have been discussed elsewhere (Eade *et al.*, 1996). Of the black groups outside of Greater London, Indians, East African Asians and Caribbeans became more concentrated in the Midlands, and

Pakistanis became more concentrated in the North West region, particularly Greater Manchester.

One corollary of such housing patterns is that, in some areas, schools tend to become racially segregated, that is, almost exclusively Asian, Caribbean or white (Bodi, 2001). Consequently, there is limited everyday interaction amongst different racial groups of young people. Whilst such trends require attention within the context of promoting better understanding between groups, it is interesting that Phil Woolas, MP for Oldham (the scene for recent civil disturbances) should feel that it is incumbent upon him to argue for the coerced integration of the Asian community (Woolas, 2001). Such sentiments are an illustration of the eurocentric perspective which continues to perceive integration as a one-way street.

In terms of patterns of tenure, the greater prevalence towards home ownership amongst Indians and Pakistanis is well recognised (Smith, 1977; Rex and Tomlinson, 1979; OPCS, 1993; Modood *et al.*, 1997). The PSI fourth survey has found that 'nearly half of Bangladeshi and Caribbean households, and more than a third of mixed Caribbean/White households, were in some form of social housing, compared with around a quarter of White and Chinese households and fewer than one out of six Indian, Pakistani and African Asian households' (Lakey, 1997, p. 200).

The poor quality of housing, including owner-occupied housing, lacking basic amenities and overcrowding are significant issues for black groups (Brown, 1984; Owen, 1993; Peach and Byron, 1993) which have an impact on family life. In the fourth PSI survey, Lakey (1997) documents high levels of housing dissatisfaction expressed by Caribbeans and Bangladeshis. She argues that this is largely because of the high proportion of council tenants among these groups. The impact of poor housing and poverty on the health situation of minority ethnic groups has been documented in research studies (Nazroo, 1997; Barn and Sidhu, 2000).

Research into housing and lone parenthood shows that lone parents are more likely to be tenants or even in temporary accommodation than their partnered counterparts (Duncan and Edwards, 1997). Moreover, they have tended to get the worst housing, for example older properties, flats rather than houses and higher floors rather than lower floors (Harrison, 1983). Peach and Byron (1993) have documented that Caribbean lone mothers fare much worse than their white counterparts in the public housing sector.

Structure of the report

Black young people constitute about 10 per cent of the total child population in Britain. The majority of these children will grow up to lead emotionally secure and healthy lives. A certain proportion will come to the attention of health and social services as a result of ill health, poverty, poor housing/homelessness, racial discrimination and disadvantage, and family breakdown, and will require help and assistance to meet their particular needs and concerns.

This report addresses the needs and concerns of those vulnerable young people who are represented amongst the statistics of 'looked after' children, the homeless, those under-achieving at school and excluded from school, young offenders, and those with substance misuse and mental health problems.

Chapter 2 explores the situation of young people in contact with the personal social services and their range of needs. A particular focus is placed on children in substitute family placements, residential care, care leavers, and those considered to be at risk of abuse and neglect.

Chapter 3 identifies some areas where black young people may be at particular risk of becoming excluded from mainstream society. Research evidence and official statistics are used to provide an understanding of the need and concerns of young people around education, employment and training, homelessness, substance misuse, juvenile justice and mental health.

Chapter 4 provides an analysis of thinking around the concept of racial and ethnic identity, and its significance to black young people in multi-racial Britain. It is argued that serious consideration also needs to be given to the ways in which white young people conceptualise and locate themselves in a racially ordered society.

Chapter 5 places its efforts in the identification of gaps for future research. This is done in the form of questions covering the different range of areas included in the main body of the report. It is hoped that the funding bodies and the research community will take heed of the gaps in current knowledge and strive to enhance understanding of the needs and concerns of minority ethnic young people with a view to securing a better future for these youngsters.

2 LOOKED AFTER YOUNG PEOPLE

There are about 50,000 children and young people looked after by local authorities in England (Department of Health, 2000). Whilst there is a statistical breakdown on a range of variables including age, gender, route of entry into care, family background and placement in care, there is no data collation of the ethnic background of these children at the national level. The Children Act Report to Parliament declares that 'ethnic monitoring will be introduced into routine statistical collections on children's services from the year 2000' (Department of Health, 2000, p. 6). It is encouraging to note central government recognises the policy and practice implications of such data collection, and it is to be hoped that such an exercise will not remain a mere data-gathering tool. The report informs us that:

> "...during 2000–2001, it will be possible to provide information on:
>
> • How ethnicity is related to the reasons for children needing help from social services
>
> • The actual services children from ethnic minorities receive and
>
> • The associated expenditure."
>
> (Department of Health, 2000, p. 6)

In the absence of national data on black children looked after by the State, this chapter provides an overview of the research findings which inform our understanding of the experiences of minority ethnic children and young people and their families in contact with social services.

Child protection

Child protection research within a mult-racial, multi-cultural perspective remains under-developed. Whilst concern has been expressed by some research studies about the high rates of referral of minority ethnic children and their subsequent registration on child protection registers (Gibbons *et al.*, 1995; Barn *et al.*, 1997), there is inadequate understanding about the circumstances which lead to referral and registration. Moreover, our knowledge and understanding about support to black families in crisis remains limited.

In addition to the chronic lack of information on the ethnicity of children looked after, actual numbers of black children and young people on social services' child protection registers are unknown. The Department of Health has collected and published statistics from all English registers since 1988; however, no information is available on the ethnicity of children. Whilst the Children Report makes mention of ethnic monitoring of children looked after, it is not clear whether such information will be recorded and collected in relation to the child protection register. It is significant to note that ethnic monitoring of children referred for child protection reasons and/or on the child protection register does not currently constitute a standardised data entry for most local authorities (Gibbons *et al.*, 1995).

There is growing concern amongst some Area Child Protection Committees (ACPCs) regarding the increasing numbers of African-

Caribbean and mixed-parentage children on their child protection registers; and, in some areas, concern is also expressed about the high numbers of Asian children in these statistics (Brent ACPC, 1997; Newham ACPC, 1998).

In a study of six local authorities in and around London and the Midlands, Gibbons *et al.* (1995) found that, whilst the proportion of black children was not inconsistent with their representations in the local population, they were over-represented among referrals for physical abuse compared to white (58 per cent compared to 42 per cent), and under-represented among referrals for sexual abuse (20 per cent compared to 31 per cent). The researchers also highlight ethnic and cultural differences in forms of child punishment; that is, black families were more often referred for using an implement, such as a cane, than white families. It was found that 43 per cent of Africans, 40 per cent of Asians and 30 per cent of African Caribbeans had beaten their children with a stick or other implement compared with 16 per cent of whites. Differences in referral agencies and their concerns regarding black and white families have been documented elsewhere (Barn, 1993; Barn *et al.*, 1997). It should be noted that Gibbons and her colleagues found that 'the consequences of the injuries inflicted on Black and Asian children were no more likely to be long-lasting', and it was 'the form the punishment took that was unacceptable to community agents who referred these children (Gibbons *et al.*, 1995, p. 40).

A study of three local authorities in London and the Midlands found a high proportion of black children on the child protection register – 60 per cent compared to 40 per cent white (Barn *et al.*, 1997). It was also found that black children were more likely to be referred for physical injury than their white counterparts and less likely to be referred for sexual abuse. Interestingly, the group most highly represented from within the black communities was Asian – 28 per cent of the children were Asian compared to 14 per cent who were African-Caribbean background, and a similar proportion who were of mixed-parentage background. Although the Asian referrals were in areas of high Asian populations in the Midlands, the study nevertheless highlighted the social construction of child abuse, and the contested nature of child protection within a framework of the differing perceptions of minority ethnic families and practitioners, and white practitioners around what constitutes 'significant harm'. It is important to note that the high rate of Asian child protection referrals did not result in care proceedings and could be argued to have been over-cautiousness on the part of the referral agencies.

Mosby *et al.* (1999) in the United States have suggested that the preference of African-American parents for physical discipline is responsible for the over-representation of black children in foster care. They found that African-American parents clearly expressed this preference to their social workers. The researchers believe that such disclosure jeopardised these parents' chances of being judged as suitable parents. It is possible that such interactions between black parents and social workers also take place in Britain; that is, black minority parents may be more likely than other parents to admit that they have physically punished their child as a means of 'correction' (Smetana, 2000).

It is important that, if child protection and family support are to be seen as a continuum (Tunstill, 1997), due regard is given to environmental and structural factors in assessment and intervention (Dutt and Phillips, 2000). It should also be noted that, although racism causes significant harm, it is not in itself a category of abuse within child protection regulations. To date, there is only one borough (London Borough of Tower Hamlets) in the country which has incorporated racial harassment as a category of abuse, alongside emotional, physical and sexual abuse and neglect. The effects of racism differ for different minority communities and individuals. It would seem to be highly important

17

that, in any assessment, the impact of racial harassment and discrimination experienced by black minority children and families is understood by social work practitioners. The situation of black mixed-parentage children and their experiences of racial harassment within their own families and in other settings also require consideration (O'Neale, 2000).

Some other areas of concern identified in qualitative research into 'race' and child protection include the complex process of using interpreters and how families may be disadvantaged in the process; a lack of holistic approach to assessment and case planning; and mental and physical health of parents (Humphries *et al.*, 1999; Chand, 2000). Research is needed into these areas as well as the general notion of 'good enough parenting' in multi-racial Britain.

Children looked after

Local authority social services departments are under a statutory duty to provide help and assistance to families to obviate family breakdown and the admission of children into the care system. Section 20 of the 1989 Children Act stipulates that local authorities will provide services to children in their area who are considered to be 'in need'. The interpretation of 'need' is at the discretion of a local authority. The legislation refers to the importance of maintaining reasonable standards in health and development, where 'health' refers to physical and mental health, and 'development' refers to physical, intellectual, emotional, social or behavioural development.

Previous research has pointed to the low levels of adequate and appropriate services to meet the needs of black families and children on the part of social services (Cheetham, 1981; Ahmed *et al.*, 1986; Barn, 1993; Caesar *et al.*, 1994). Moreover, the numbers of black children have been shown to be high in the public care system. Some early research in the mid-1950s carried out by the National Children's Home initiated concern about the plight of minority children in the care system and identified practice considerations (National Children's Home, 1954). It is possible that some of these minority children included 'black war babies', that is, mixed-parentage children born of white mothers and African-American GI fathers during the Second World War (Baker, 1999).

In 1958, the Family Welfare Association reported that the problems of minority families were no different to those of the indigenous population and that they were making adequate use of services. Subsequent studies highlighted the problem of a growing number of black children in residential homes and the difficulties of finding substitute families for these children (Rowe and Lambert, 1973). Much of the early research adopted a problematic approach, and focused on minority family structures and lifestyles to understand the situation of these families (Fitzherbert, 1967; McCulloch *et al.*, 1979). It appears that there was little or no attempt to explore the impact of structural racism on minority family life, and the relevance or appropriateness of British social work theory and practice. The negative over-emphasis on minority family structures and lifestyles has led to a paradigm of deficit within social work which is now in need of a major and significant challenge (Small, 1984; Barn, 2000, 2001; Rashid and Rashid, 2000). The illusory norms of eurocentric thinking require serious debate within the increasing racial and cultural heterogeneity of British society.

Contributory factors leading to high admission rates

Research evidence over the last five decades has indicated the high representation of black children in the care system (National Children's Home, 1954; Fitzherbert, 1967; Pinder and Shaw, 1974;

19

McCulloch *et al.*, 1979, Bebbington and Miles, 1989, Rowe *et al.*, 1989, Barn, 1993; Barn *et al.*, 1997). Contributory factors put forward to explain the high admission rates of black children into public care include high birth rate, geographical concentration, family breakdown, lack of preventative work with families and institutional racism (Boss and Homeshaw, 1974; Pinder and Shaw, 1974; Commission for Racial Equality, 1978; Batta and Mawby, 1981; Barn, 1993).

It appears that some of factors put forward in the academic literature have arisen not so much from empirical research, but largely from conjecture. For example, the high birth rate factor does not hold up to scrutiny. As mentioned in Chapter 1, the largest black group in Britain is Indian, followed by African Caribbean and Pakistani. The two groups with the highest numbers of young people are Pakistani and Bangladeshi (4.8 and 5.3 respectively per household). Yet, research tells us that the two groups highly represented in the public care system include Caribbean and those of mixed Caribbean/white parentage (Bebbington and Miles, 1989; Rowe *et al.*, 1989; Barn, 1993; Barn *et al.*, 1997). Indeed, research has consistently indicated the low representation of Asian children in the care system (Rowe *et al.*, 1989; Barn, 1993; Barn *et al.*, 1997).

The arguments around geographical concentration and supposed family dysfunctionality need to be understood within a wider context of disadvantage and discrimination. As discussed in the introductory chapter, minority groups have suffered disproportionately in terms of poor housing and unemployment. The ability of families to cope is hampered by such adverse conditions. To describe such difficulties as family dysfunctionality is to fail to understand the circumstances of families and the impact of poor environments (Ghate, 2000). The author's own research has shown that, in one inner-city London borough, a high proportion of the families in contact with social services were living in local authority housing, and that poor and overcrowded housing was often a concern for African-Caribbean families (Barn, 1993). Our research shows that significantly more black children were admitted into care where poor housing was a contributory factor – 10 per cent black compared to 4 per cent white, $p <$ 0.004 (Barn, 1993). The majority of black children were of African-Caribbean and mixed-parentage backgrounds.

Lack of preventive work with families; and institutionalised racism in social work education and training, and policy and practice have been identified as contributory factors leading to the high admission rates of black children in care, and their subsequent negative experiences and placement outcomes (Barn, 1993; Barn et al., 1997).

Clearly, no single factor is sufficient in developing an understanding of the complexity involved in black families' experiences of social services. Whilst it is useful to explore the various arguments, it is essential that these arguments are refuted or supported by sound empirical research. The paucity of research in the areas of 'race', ethnicity and social work is such that our knowledge base in relation to minority families and social care remains largely under-developed.

Rapid entry into care

Research evidence shows that some black groups are much more vulnerable and susceptible to entering the public care system at times of crisis. Moreover, such crisis situations are referred to the social services by statutory agencies such as education, health and the police rather than by families themselves (Barn, 1993; Barn et al., 1997). It would appear that, by the time families are referred for help, preventive strategies are either under-employed or fail to be effective. Barn et al. (1997) found that African-Caribbean children were twice as likely to enter care in the early stages compared to their white counterparts. They were also more likely to spend longer periods in care than white children. Barn *et al.* (1997) documented that one in three looked after African-Caribbean children remained in the care system for more than five years compared to one in ten white children. Research is needed to explore the qualitative experiences of black young people in the care system and to explore the reasons for their lengthy stays in care.

Foster care

The numbers of black children in foster care, at a national level, remains unknown. Research studies over the years have pointed to the difficulties of finding appropriate substitute family placements for black children and have shown black children to be 'hard to place' in family settings (Rowe and Lambert, 1973). The realisation of the negative effects of transracial placements (Divine, 1983; Gill and Jackson, 1983; Small, 1984) contributed to changes in child-care legislation to consider the racial and ethnic background of children looked after.

The 1989 Children Act, sec. 22(5)(c) identified the importance of four elements:

- 'race'
- culture
- religion
- language.

Recognition of these four elements by local authority social services departments has been varied. The author's own research in this area has shown that, where local authorities have invested adequate resources, certain minority ethnic group children have a good chance of being placed in foster family settings and, more specifically, in families which reflect the child's own racial and cultural background (Barn, 1993; Barn *et al.*, 1997). It was found that there were at times crude attempts at racial matching as a result of a lack of comprehensive assessment of the child's needs and concerns. As a consequence, black foster carers were placed in difficult situations and given little preparation and support. Such practice does not lend itself to the retention of foster carers and creates difficulties in meeting placement needs. A recent study by the Family Rights Group has documented the continual practice of transracial placements by local authorities, and ad hoc progress in equal opportunity and anti-discriminatory matters (Richards and Ince, 2000).

Mixed-parentage children present a placement dilemma for social services. The vast majority of mixed-parentage children who enter the care system come from a single-parent family. In such cases, the single parent tends to be the white birth mother and the absent father African Caribbean. The mixed-parentage child may have little or no contact with their black relatives.

It should be noted that the recording of mixed ethnicity in social services records is also an area of contention. It is possible that only the 'visible' mixed ethnicity children and young people are recorded as mixed-parentage, thereby reinforcing the black/white divide. Racial classification of individuals is more than mere data gathering, it is highly politicised. The policy, practice and provision implications of racialised data are yet to be realised.

Barn *et al.* (1997) found that mixed-parentage children were equally likely to be placed with a black or a white family. Thus, whilst Caribbean and Asian children would be placed in families which reflected their own racial and cultural background, it was not clear where mixed-parentage children should be placed. Social work practitioners grappled with questions such as: is a mixed-parentage child in a white substitute family seen to be in a transracial family, particularly given that they were being looked after by their white birth mother before admission into care? The categorisation on the basis of 'race' and ethnicity, and the practices of 'same race' and transracial placements required more complex thinking in the situation of children whose ethnic background was 'mixed', and thus challenged the boundaries of racialised identities. Barn *et al.* (1997) noted that placement decisions with regard to mixed-parentage children were, at times, being made within simplistic notions of 'race' and colour. For example, factors such as skin shade were taken as an indicator of where the child should be placed rather than the long-term needs of the child within a holistic and ecological framework.

Ince (1998) highlights the impact of transracial placements on black young people's racial identity. She found that five of the black young people in her sample of ten perceived themselves to be white while growing up in care. Because of a lack of racial/cultural input from white foster/adoptive parents, and from social services, and to a lack of contact with black people, these young people showed a resistance to 'mixing' with black people, and held negative views about them.

There is little research evidence about the quality of foster placements in relation to black children. Thoburn and Rowe (1991) showed that mixed-parentage children were more likely to be in a placement which disrupted than other black or white children. Some of the positive factors identified by researchers which may lead to stability and security for black children include regular contact with birth parents and/or sibling(s) placed elsewhere, understanding and empathy from foster carer (Barn, 1993; Barn *et al.*, 1997), and placement with a sibling (Thoburn and Rowe, 1991). However, there is little research evidence to demonstrate the risk and protective factors in child-care placements and how these might be experienced by different ethnic groups.

Residential care

There is a lack of recent research exploring the experiences of black children in residential care. A number of studies have documented the high representation of black youngsters in residential institutions (Lambert, 1970; Rowe and Lambert, 1973; Pearce, 1974; Cawson, 1977). Lambert (1970) in his study of Birmingham community homes found that a number of Asian, African-Caribbean and mixed-parentage youngsters entered such units because of family conflicts. In a study of 125 approved schools, Pearce (1974) found that African-Caribbean boys were 'over-represented in Community Home Schools, possibly as a result of differential police activity' (Pearce, 1974, p. 323).

The experiences of black children in residential care institutions is a much neglected area. In 1979, a Commission for Racial Equality (CRE) report pointed out that the basic cultural needs of black children were not being adequately met. Barn (1993) has shown that the eurocentric ethos of residential homes and the lack of black staff leads to a low level of awareness of the needs and concerns of black children.

Racist bullying and racial harassment from staff and other residents has been documented in the literature (Pinder, 1982; Black and In Care, 1984). It was found that staff in residential homes had little or no understanding of black cultures and experiences in this country. This resulted in staff incompetence in resolving racial conflicts within the institution, or presumably the concerns of young people arising from external sources, for example, in schools.

Barn (1993) found that children placed in residential homes within their own multi-racial, multi-cultural locality had a positive racial and ethnic identity as a result of regular contact with their own community and birth family, and as a result of the positive influences made by black residential staff. In a study on racial identity attitudes and self-esteem amongst black (African-Caribbean) young people in residential care, and those in the community, Robinson (2000) found relatively high levels of self-esteem and internalisation (positive racial) attitudes. Robinson suggests that the predominance of such attitudes among young black people in residential care could be linked to the inner-city multi-racial location of the residential homes, and the positive racial attitudes of their care workers, the majority of whom were black.

Adoption

A Department of Health audit report summarising seven local authority inspections in 1996 found that placement patterns for black children were varied (Social Services Inspectorate, 1997). The report documents that local authorities were not rigidly pursuing same-race placement policies. In fact, the majority of black children were placed in white families (see Table 3). The report also identified delays in the placement of both black and white children, and urged local authorities to act quickly in the best interests of children. Recent national research carried out by the British Agencies for Adoption and Fostering support the Department of Health (DoH) findings with respect to the adoptive placement of black children (Invaldi, 2000).

Table 3 Placement of minority ethnic children

Placement	Number of cases	Percentage of total
Placed with white families	30	53.5
Placed with dual race heritage families	7	12.5
Placed with minority ethnic families	19	34.0
Total	56	100.0

Source: Social Services Inspectorate, 1997, p. 27

In line with the requirements of the 1989 Children Act, the report states that, 'All things being equal, the preferred placement for a child from an ethnic minority is with a family with the same racial and cultural background' (Social Services Inspectorate, 1997, p. 28). With regard to transracial placement of black children, the report places the onus upon social services departments (SSDs) to establish that the placement choice is the preferred one. It is curious that, although the Government's own audit highlights the majority of adoptions of black children as transracial, Paul Boateng, the former Junior Health Minister, should have attacked local authorities for pursuing same-race adoptions (Boateng, 1998). Paul Boateng's criticism of social work agencies resulted in a 'Local Authority Circular' highlighting the Government's impatience with the 'race' principal (Department of Health, 1998). Whilst reinforcing the underlying ethos around 'race' and ethnicity embedded in the 1989 Children Act, sec. 22(5)(c), the Circular links into the delay findings of the SSI report and states:

"The Government has made it clear that it is unacceptable for a child to be denied loving adoptive parents solely on the grounds that the child and adopters do not share the same racial or cultural background."
(Department of Health, 1998)

The placement needs of black children have, hitherto, been debated within the political framework of the day. The political ideology of the 1960s set the scene within an integrationist framework where the ultimate goal was one of racial harmony. Research evidence about the upbringing of transracially adopted black young people informs us about the one way and parochial nature of such thinking. Minority children were welcomed into white homes, but they were expected to think and behave as the adoptive family, and not see themselves as racially different. Lack of contact with people of their own racial and cultural background, with little or no input about their racial and cultural heritage, meant that these youngsters grew up believing themselves to be 'white in all but skin colour' (Gill and Jackson, 1983, p. 81). The outcome of such a cocooned upbringing meant that, as children and later as adults, these individuals were culturally bereft and ill-equipped to come to terms with their own racial identity, and to deal with 'race' and racism in society.

The notions of belonging and identity play a crucial role in the lives of every individual. In racially and culturally fractured societies, belonging and identity exercise an important influence. The role of the minority ethnic parent in ensuring that their offspring are able to develop a healthy identification with people of their own ethnic background and to deal with a discriminatory society is crucial. At present, there is little research which can tell us about the ability of white substitute parents to competently raise black children. Much of the previous research, both from the UK and US, gives cause for concern in the task of racial and cultural input.

There is research literature from both the United States and from Britain which shows that transracial placements result in black children having a poor self-concept and a negative racial identity (Simon and Alstein, 1981; Gill and Jackson, 1983; Shireman and Johnson, 1986). Interestingly, much of this research has been presented by the researchers and used by proponents of transracial placements to lend credence to the continued practice of transracial placements. High educational performance at school has been seen as the primary indicator of success, whilst worrying findings around racial identity have been underplayed.

The difficulties faced by white substitute parents in ensuring that black children grow up in an environment where they develop a positive sense of their own racial and cultural identity have been highlighted in the British literature. A recent study into permanent family placements where two-thirds of the children were of mixed parentage has documented differences between black and white long-term foster carers (Thoburn et al., 1998). The study found that 'whilst some White families can successfully parent children who are of a different ethnic origin from themselves, they have extra obstacles to surmount in ensuring that the young people have a positive sense of themselves as members of a particular ethnic group' (Thoburn et al., 1998, p. 159). In a study of the Post-adoption Centre in London, Howe and Hinings (1987) found that white adoptive parents to black children tended to be over-represented amongst those seeking help and advice. Clearly, these families were in a crisis and needed support. In a study of 274 black children who were placed with black foster or adoptive parents, Charles et al. (1992) found that these children were on average older and were more likely to have emotional or behavioural difficulties at the time of placement.

In their review on the outcome of transracial placements, Rushton and Minnis (1997) concluded that breakdown rates seem to be determined by age rather than type of placement. They argue that the development outcomes of transracially placed children appear to be good for the majority in terms of education attainment, peer relations and behaviour. In a recent paper, they suggest that, in situations where transracial placements are the only option, then consideration needs to be given to placing children in multi-ethnic communities, and that support and training should be provided for the substitute families (Rushton and Minnis, 2000).

The recent revisitation of the debates around transracial versus same race have arisen from high-profile media cases such as that of Jim and Roma Laurence, an inter-racial couple from East Anglia who were deemed unsuitable as adopters because of their apparent 'racial naivety'. Postmodern thinking around changing ethnic identities in new and developing contexts is also an influential contributor to such debates. The reality is that, as long as we continue to have racial divisions in society, and racial and cultural hierarchies, the debates around the best substitute placement for black children living in such societies will continue.

At present, there is little research evidence about the relative experiences of black youngsters in substitute care. Research into the relative contributions of black and white substitute carers would identify areas of strengths and concern. Such research would be invaluable not in political or ideological ways, but in terms of policy and practice for local authorities, practitioners, carers and, in the long run, in the interests of black young people.

Care leavers

About 8,000 young people leave the care system each year (British Youth Council, 1998). Evans (1996) documented that, whilst 1 per cent of children and young people have been in care, between 20 and 50 per cent of young homeless people have been in care. Moreover, research studies have shown care leavers to be significantly disadvantaged in education, employment and training, and links between care and mental health problems and young offenders have also been made.

The high number of black young people in the care system and the likelihood of these youngsters spending lengthy periods in care has been documented (Bebbington and Miles, 1989; Rowe *et al.*, 1989; Barn, 1993; Barn *et al.*, 1997). Consequently, black young people are highly represented amongst those leaving care at the end of their care career aged 16–18.

In 1987, First Key undertook an empirical study of black young people leaving care. Based on data collected in interviews and formal questionnaires with 54 young people and staff from

'Preparation for Independence' projects in three London boroughs, the study expressed concern around type and location of placement and its impact on young people's cultural identity. The study documented that, where youngsters had been fostered by white families living in predominantly white neighbourhoods, or where young people were placed in residential homes where the staff were predominantly white, this led to a low level of cultural awareness and resulted in young people being confused about their cultural identity. Such lack of awareness led to a low level of confidence and self-esteem which was an added burden at the time of leaving care.

The First Key study identified the problems experienced by black young people moving from a white environment to meeting other people of black background:

> "They face pressure from their Black peer group who expect them to know their culture and from White social workers with their own expectations. And they face the added element of racism ... they may have often been cared for in a way which ignores they are Black; when they move out of care, it is impossible for them to ignore it."
>
> (First Key, 1987, p. 7)

The study made a number of recommendations including the recruitment of black staff and carers, working in partnership with minority communities and projects, and the development of equal opportunities and anti-racism policies.

With the exception of one small qualitative study, there has been no systematic research carried out to evaluate the specific experiences of black young people leaving the care system (Ince, 1998). Ince's study based on interviews with ten black care leavers highlights the impact of direct and indirect discrimination and suggests that the problems of isolation, loneliness, homelessness, unemployment, poor education, and a lack of information and advice are heightened by such experiences. The impact of lengthy stays in the care system, documented in other research (Barn, 1993; Barn et al., 1997), and isolation and lack of contact with the black family and community are identified by Ince as pervading factors leading to difficulties around ethnic and cultural identity for black young people in the care system.

Other research studies into care leavers have included small numbers of black care leavers, and it would be misleading to generalise from such work (Garnett, 1992; Biehal et al., 1995). Research evidence is needed about the qualitative experiences of black young people to determine their needs and concerns, and how these are being met by service providers.

The Children Act 1989 (sec. 24) makes it a clear duty of local authorities to advise, assist and befriend the young person with a view to promoting his/her welfare when he/she ceases to be looked after by them. The disadvantage and discrimination facing black young people in relation to education, employment and housing have been documented by previous research. The experiences of black young people leaving the care system warrant urgent research attention. The social costs of not preparing young people in the care system for post-care life are immense. Research studies have commented that such preparation should be an ongoing activity, and not merely six months before departure from care (First Key, 1987).

3 OTHER VULNERABLE GROUPS

This chapter explores a range of areas where black young people may be at particular risk and vulnerability. A review of the research literature shows that, by and large, the issues and concerns facing black young people remain unexplored. It is of concern that major texts on youth and social exclusion fail to incorporate issues of 'race' and racism. A passing reference made to a few studies for drawing 'attention to the diverse and changing cultural responses developed by Black youth to the racial discrimination and class disadvantage they experience' is inadequate (Macdonald, 1997, p. 192). It is encouraging to note, however, that some research studies are beginning to explore the circumstances of young people from a range of different ethnic backgrounds to highlight the similarities and differences in the availability and use of services and opportunities (Nassor and Simms, 1996; Wade *et al.*, 1998).

Education, employment and training

There is an inextricable link between education and employment. Employment chances are greatly determined by educational attainment and training. Young people who leave school with few or no qualifications have a much poorer capability of securing employment than their counterparts.

As mentioned in Chapter 1, the black population has a much younger age structure than the white population, representing nearly 12 per cent of primary school pupils and around 11 per cent of secondary school pupils in England (Department for Education and Employment, 1999). Projections for the next decade show that the most rapid increase in the working-age population will occur amongst black other (who tend to be younger-generation African Caribbeans and those of mixed parentage), Bangladeshis, Pakistanis and Africans (Metcalf and Forth, 2000).

Education

Over the last few decades, there has been considerable debate and discussion in the areas of 'race', ethnicity and schooling in Britain. Amongst the development of concepts such as 'multi-cultural' and 'anti-racist' education, one issue – 'under-achievement' – has dominated research and policy (Rampton, 1981; Swann, 1985). Indeed, the documentation of inequality of opportunity and the resultant 'under-achievement' by some black groups has been the driving force behind 'multi-cultural', and anti-racist education. The impact of such initiatives over the last two decades has been regarded, by some, as piecemeal and largely ineffective (Tomlinson, 1987; Troyna, 1987).

Under-achievement

The term 'under-achievement' has been employed over the last two decades to denote differential educational attainment amongst ethnic groups (Rampton, 1981; Swann, 1985). Gillborn and Mirza (2000) argue that, although information about differential attainment and ethnicity is important in understanding inequalities in educational outcomes, care should be taken to avoid a racially hierarchical view based on assumptions of inherent ability.

Research evidence over the last few decades has consistently shown some black young people, notably African Caribbean, Pakistani and Bangladeshi, to under-achieve in schools (Rampton, 1981; Swann, 1985; Eggleston et al., 1986).

Research into gender differences within under-achieving groups is limited. There is some evidence to show that girls in general (from all major ethnic groups) are more likely to achieve five or more higher-grade GCSEs than boys from the same ethnic group (Department for Education and Employment, 1999; Demack et al., 2000). However, it seems that the inequalities of attainment of Bangladeshi/Pakistani and African-Caribbean girls mean not only that they do less well than white and Indian girls, but also that they are less likely to attain five higher-grade GCSEs than white and Indian boys (Gillborn and Mirza, 2000).

It is significant to note that there are no national statistics available on individual pupil achievement. Data from individual local education authorities and nationally representative surveys reveal important differences in achievement at the early key stages and at GCSE level. Ofsted (1999) documented that black pupils, and African-Caribbean boys in particular, perform less well than white pupils in early schooling and make least progress through school. Low attainment amongst Bangladeshi and Pakistani pupils has also been highlighted (Gillborn and Gipps, 1996; Ofsted, 1999). Under-achievement among African-Caribbean, Pakistani and Bangladeshi pupils continues at GCSE level. In contrast, Indian and some other Asian (including Chinese) pupils do very well, outperforming other pupils.

Factors that may contribute to under-achievement are identified as social class, child's cultural background, neighbourhood, peer and teacher influence and school effectiveness (Gillborn and Gipps, 1996; Department for Education and Employment, 1999). Gillborn and Gipps (1996) highlight lack of fluency in English as one significant factor leading to the early under-achievement of

Pakistani and Bangladeshi pupils. However, given that research informs us that other pupils with early fluency difficulties do make substantial progress, it is not clear why Pakistani and Bangladeshi pupils perform poorly at GCSE level. Gillborn and Gipps (1996) argue that the negative school experiences of some African-Caribbean boys appear to be an important element in their academic under-achievement.

Luthra (1997, p. 193) believes that research into comparative under-achievement, as opposed to relative progression, has led to a 'victimology of its own thus catalysing the culture of failure within the same groups'. Such a framework has hampered research from a holistic perspective exploring the range of influences and the actual progression of different groups. Research evidence from cohort studies on assessment from junior to secondary schools suggests that, although the differential patterns of achievement are established during early years of schooling, some groups, particularly African-Caribbean boys, slide back whilst others are able to exceed at secondary level (Sammons, 1994).

School exclusion

There is little doubt that school exclusion has an adverse effect on young people's education and their subsequent life chances. Recent research documents that boys are significantly more likely to be excluded from school than girls, for example, boys accounted for 83 per cent of the permanent exclusions in 1995–96 (Department for Education and Employment, 1997). Within this group, Ofsted and the Department for Education and Employment (DfEE) have shown that African-Caribbean boys are four to six times more likely to be excluded than their white counterparts. Majors *et al.* (1998) argue that, in the absence of national statistics on fixed-term exclusions, it is likely that the official statistics under-estimate the true level of exclusions among black boys. Moreover, it is feared that black boys may be highly represented in 'informal' or 'back-door' exclusions, for instance where parents are asked to withdraw their child before a formal exclusion can occur (Majors *et al.*, 1998).

Circumstances under which African-Caribbean boys become excluded appear to be anchored in a 'race' and ethnicity framework. As mentioned above, research evidence over the last two decades has pointed to the under-achievement levels of African-Caribbean boys, and the role of racism as a contributory factor in schools and in society at large (Rampton, 1981; Swann, 1985; Eggleston *et al.*, 1986). Low expectations on the part of teachers and negative stereotyping of black boys have been shown to be an important factor (Eggleston *et al.*, 1986; Wright, 1987). *The Black Child Report* (1999–2000) found that 22 per cent of black young people they sampled felt they had been subjected to racism from the teachers over the previous four weeks. This is higher than the perceived racism from classmates. Parsons (1996) found that different peer and teacher influences may increase African-Caribbean boys' resistance to school, leading to serious disciplinary responses such as exclusion. Moreover, once excluded, the majority are unlikely to return to mainstream education, thus being further disadvantaged.

Research studies have found that black boys are often excluded from schools for exhibiting 'culture-specific' behaviours (for example, hair styles, eye behaviour, walking styles) in the classroom (Majors *et al.*, 1998). It would appear that black boys are less likely to be over-monitored, disregarded or harassed by teachers when they deny their cultural identity and display assimilationist tendencies (Fordham, 1996; Sewell, 1997). Majors *et al.* (1998) argue that a school becomes a battleground in which black boys seek recognition and affirmation of their racial and cultural identity. Exclusion would appear to be one aspect of such tension between teachers and black boys. Such an environment is clearly not conducive to learning and good educational attainment.

In a study of young people going missing from the care system, Wade *et al.* (1998) found high rates of non-school attendance and school exclusion. The researchers found that, in their main survey of 210 children which included 42 black young people, over two-fifths of those of school age were not attending school, and many of these were excluded from school. However, Wade *et al.* (1998) found no significant relationship between school exclusion and ethnic origin. They argue that patterns of school exclusion are so strongly associated with emotional and behavioural difficulties including offending that this overrides any association with ethnic origin (Wade *et al.*, 1998). It is important to understand, however, that school exclusion documentation is unlikely to over-emphasise 'race' and ethnicity for fear of being seen as racist, and that conscious and unconscious racism may be cloaked in what are described as emotional and behavioural problems. Research exploring the significance of 'race' and ethnicity in school exclusions is required to explore empirically the impact of these factors in school dynamics.

Powis *et al.* (1998) express concern about the long-term outcomes of pupils excluded from school and their possible increasing involvement in drug use and crime. In a London-based study of 86 school excludees, aged 14–16, attending Pupil Referral Units (education centres for young people excluded from schools), the researchers found that half of the sample group were from black backgrounds, most lived in single-parent families and nearly two-thirds had no adult wage earner. Almost all of the young people had committed a criminal offence, with a third having committed an assault or wounding and nearly a third having committed a burglary. It was also found that levels of lifetime and current drug use were high, and the range of drugs used was wide.

Following the suicide of Jevan Richardson, a ten-year-old pupil who was excluded from school in Lewisham, South London, there has been some media attention given to the under-achievement and school exclusion of black pupils. The Richardson family have launched a campaign protesting over the death of Jevon, and are seeking to sue the school and Lewisham educational authority for what they consider to have been an 'illegal' exclusion (Woodward, 2001). Future media attention and the success of this case could become an important watershed in highlighting the situation of worryingly high numbers of exclusions of black young people.

Although there is little documented research evidence to signify the school exclusion of Asian youth (see Mayet, 1993), there is recognition of the problem in some areas. The London Borough of Tower Hamlets, for example, has set up a multi-agency preventative project to work with Bangladeshi boys who may be under-achieving and who may be or are at risk of school exclusion. The project employs youth workers, social workers and clinical psychologists to work with the youngsters and their families. The efficacy of such joint-working needs to be highlighted and shared amongst the health and social care professionals for the betterment of disaffected young people (MAP, 2000).

Pathak (2000) documents that there is anecdotal information from schools and local agencies that community mentoring has a positive impact on minority pupils. In the absence of empirical evidence, the relative merits of such an approach remain unknown. Research into this area exploring the benefits of mentors for black pupils would enhance our understanding of the importance of such schemes.

Although the impact of gender is being realised, few schools use ethnic monitoring to track attainment and raise standards. Research shows that a good school, with a strong leadership and tracking systems will benefit all pupils, regardless of ethnic origin (Ofsted, 1999). Research in this area will be important to measure the impact of such tracking and other innovative strategies.

The problems of under-achievement, institutional racism, school exclusion and racial bullying in schools require urgent attention. Whilst some within the black communities have sought to address such problems by establishing separate schools along the lines of faith schools, others continue to battle with the mainstream to bring about positive change. There is a considerable body of research evidence to begin to effect some change. Multi-cultural and anti-racist education has proved to be little more than rhetoric, and has been perceived to be ill-thought out, piecemeal, directed at black young people and largely responsible for creating racial divisions between black and white pupils (Nayak, 1999). It would appear that the failure of central government to require a culturally relevant curriculum for all, and to make concerted efforts to train and appoint black teachers who could act as role models results in British black young people feeling marginalised in a society which gives little positive recognition to diversity.

Employment and training

The incidence of high unemployment rates amongst black young people has been documented in research studies (Drew *et al.*, 1992). However, different patterns of participation in full-time education prevent a clear picture of patterns of unemployment amongst young people from different ethnic groups.

Modood *et al.* (1997) found that young males between the ages of 16 and 19 were broadly represented in two categories; that is, the unemployment rates for whites and Indian/African Asians was around a third, while Caribbeans and Pakistani/

Bangladeshis had rates over a half. For women in this age group, the rate of unemployment amongst whites was a quarter compared to about a half for other black groups.

Research evidence suggests that young people who leave full-time education at an early age (that is, prior to taking GCSEs and A levels) to enter the labour market may be poorly equipped to compete for jobs (Payne, 1996). Modood *et al.* (1997) found that most of the small minority of young Asian people who did not stay on at school were poorly qualified to compete for jobs, both compared with older Asians and economically active members of other ethnic groups.

Research evidence shows that young people from all black groups are more likely to stay on at school after the minimum leaving age than white young people (Berthoud, 1999). In contrast, white young people are more likely to be in employment and government-supported training than ethnic minorities. In a comparison of the qualifications achieved by those who stayed on at each stage, Berthoud (1999) found variations in the time taken by different groups to achieve the same qualifications. For example, African-Caribbean young men required half a year longer in the education system, on average, to achieve the same qualifications as white men. African and Indian young men required a full additional year. Pakistani and Bangladeshi young men had to study for two additional years to obtain their qualifications compared with white men.

There is evidence to show that, despite a high participation rate in further education, a significant proportion of Bangladeshis and Pakistanis are not in education, training or employment (14 per cent and 9 per cent respectively compared to 6 per cent of whites) (Department for Education and Employment, 1999). Black young people, aged 16–24, are also consistently less likely than their white counterparts to be on Work Based Training for Young

People. Evidence shows that those on Work Based Training for Young People are more likely to be on lower-level programmes such as Other Training (OT) and National Traineeships (NTr) than Modern Apprenticeships (MA) (Department for Education and Employment, 1999).

It would appear that black young people are less likely than their white counterparts to move from the New Deal Employment Scheme to permanent jobs, despite having better qualifications (Ward, 2000). Evidence shows that Bangladeshi (37 per cent), Black African (39 per cent) and Pakistani (39 per cent) young people on OT are much less likely to be in employment compared to 63 per cent of white participants (Department for Education and Employment, 1999). Black groups on MA are more successful in obtaining jobs, but they are still less likely than white young people to be in employment after training (70 per cent of black young people and 73 per cent of Asians are in employment compared to 84 per cent of white MA leavers).

In an analysis of 11 years of the Labour Force Surveys, Berthoud (1999) made three observations in relation to levels of unemployment amongst young people (aged 16–39).

- White and Indian young people were at a relatively low risk of unemployment.

- Pakistanis and Bangladeshis were at a high risk of unemployment.

- Africans and African Caribbeans were at an average risk of unemployment, but there were strong variations within the group depending on individual characteristics. However, it was found that African young men suffered severe disadvantage in spite of educational success.

Berthoud (1999) found that unemployment was much higher among teenage minority ethnic men. More than 40 per cent of 16–17 year olds from black groups were unemployed compared with only 18 per cent of whites. High teenage unemployment rates were closely associated with the lack of qualifications obtained by early leavers.

It would appear that, whilst we have some quantitative data on education, employment and training patterns of minority ethnic young people, we know little of their qualitative experience. Future research needs to explore the experiences of young people to understand disparities between black and white groups, but also amongst different minority ethnic groups.

Homelessness

In understanding the size and nature of the problem of homelessness amongst black young people, it is important to take into account various methodological issues; for example, the ways in which 'homelessness' is defined, the location of research studies and the categorisation of ethnic groupings.

A national survey of homelessness in urban areas found that almost 20 per cent of the young homeless population were from ethnic minorities (Smith, 1999). Other surveys have shown that nearly half (48 per cent) of those admitted to Centrepoint's London hostels are from minority ethnic groups (Nassor and Simms, 1996). In 1993, a study of single homeless people found that over a third of those under 25 were from a minority ethnic background (Anderson, 1993).

Smith (1999) documents that the inner London boroughs have a much higher proportion of black young people among their homeless population. She found that nearly one in five young people were of African-Caribbean origin (19 per cent), one in seven were of African origin (14 per cent) and one in 20 were of Asian origin. Smith also found that young black women were more likely to be homeless than their white counterparts. Among homeless young women, 44 per cent were white compared to 24 per cent African Caribbean, 16 per cent African and 5 per cent Asian. The reverse was true in the case of black young men. Among young homeless men, 58 per cent were white (British, Irish and European) compared to 16 per cent African Caribbean, 13 per cent African and 5 per cent Asian. It is important to point out that one in six of the young homeless people in London included young African refugees. Smith (1999) found that, despite being over-represented among the homeless population, young women and men of African-Caribbean origin were under-represented among the rough sleeping population, and were more likely to report that they had stayed the previous night with friends and relatives. Smith suggests that threats of violence and harassment may be contributory factors in the low representation of African-Caribbean young people amongst the rough sleepers.

In a study of 126 young people aged 16–25, Davies and Lyle (1996) found that, although the most common cause of homelessness among young people from all ethnic groups is family breakdown, Caribbean and Asian homeless people are less likely to have been asked to leave home and more likely to have stayed with friends or relatives than their white counterparts. It is also of interest to note that the researchers encountered considerable difficulty in contacting homeless Asian young people. This was said to be common to all three case study areas (West Yorkshire, the West Midlands and the East Midlands). Davies and Lyle suggest that this led from 'a reluctance on the part of Asian communities to recognise that youth homelessness was a significant problem and an insistence that homelessness which did exist was dealt with by and within the community' (Davies and Lyle, 1996, p. 6). It is also possible that, given the low number of Asian young homeless people in the study, researchers were not able to recruit sufficient numbers for interview. The study found that white young people were most likely to turn to statutory and voluntary agencies for support, whilst Caribbean young homeless people were less likely and Asian young homeless people were least likely of all. Despite these differing rates of help-seeking, nearly half of all young people who approached homelessness agencies in England and Northern Ireland during 1994/95 were from minority ethnic groups (Nassor and Simms, 1996).

It would appear that running away from home as a child may also be a common precursor to homelessness. In one study, 53 per cent of homeless young people interviewed had run away from home or care before the age of 16 and 85 per cent had run away on more than one occasion (Craig et al., 1997). Research evidence into black young people running away from home and from public care has shown that there is an over-representation of African-Caribbean young people and an under-representation of those of Asian background (Abrahams and Mungall, 1992; Rees, 1993). Abrahams and Mungall (1992) found that a quarter of all runaways from substitute care in London were of African-Caribbean origin. More recent research contradicts previous studies in documenting that levels of running away are similar across minority ethnic groups (Children's Society, 1999). However, it highlights another worrying trend that African-Caribbean and Asian young people (41 per cent and 34 per cent respectively) are significantly more likely to stay away for a week or more than white young people (18 per cent). Reasons for this are unclear and need exploration.

In their study of school excludees in four local authorities in London, the Midlands and the North, Wade et al. (1998) documented that a fifth of their sample in their main survey and a quarter of their community homes sample were young people from a minority ethnic background, predominantly African Caribbean and those of mixed African Caribbean/white origin. Since African-Caribbean and mixed-parentage young people constitute the largest group of black young people in public care, it is not surprising to learn that they are highly represented in the runaway statistics in comparison to young people of Asian background (Bebbington and Miles, 1989; Rowe *et al.*, 1989; Barn, 1993; Barn *et al.*, 1997).

From interviews with young people who had run away from care homes, including nine black young people (predominantly those of mixed Caribbean/white parentage) and 27 white young people, Wade *et al.* (1998) conclude that 'Black and White young people are not likely to go missing for different reasons', although racist bullying was a factor for two of the black young people interviewed in the study (p. 40). Based on interviews with black young people, social workers and residential workers, they report that, while there is no manifest link between patterns of absence and motivations for going missing and 'race', some black young people were 'more likely to return to support networks in their home areas while missing rather than head for the city centre streets, where they would be more visible and more likely to experience racist abuse' (Wade *et al.*, 1998, p. 40). It is significant to note that, in a study of 564 children looked after in one inner-city London local authority, the author found that black children (predominantly African Caribbean and those of Caribbean/white mixed parentage) enjoyed more frequent contact with their birth families than white children (Barn, 1993). Such regular contact would be conducive to black young people choosing to return to their home areas as opposed to heading for the strangeness of city centre streets.

Children and young people are also affected by the homelessness of families. A report into the health of rehoused families in the London Borough of Tower Hamlets found that 50–

60 per cent of the statutory homeless are Bangladeshi. The families were also more likely to remain homeless for longer periods than other groups, and were generally more disadvantaged in terms of housing and health. Disruption in children's education was also a key issue. It was found that 45 per cent of households had children who had missed periods of schooling due to homelessness and nearly half of these had missed up to one year of school. Bangladeshi schoolchildren in Tower Hamlets are less likely to have qualifications or to stay on at school after the age of 16 (Sen and Zaman, 1992). Mobility and lack of continuity in education have serious health implications, including missing out on screening programmes, development, medical and dental checks.

Research evidence shows that black young people are increasingly represented among homeless young people. Homelessness may be as a result of young people leaving their family following family breakdown, running away from the care system, or as a result of families becoming homeless. It would appear that whilst we know something about the size of the problem, we know little about the circumstances that lead to homelessness, and the qualitative experiences of accessing support services (Julienne, 1998).

Substance misuse

Research into the nature and extent of substance misuse amongst black groups in general, and black young people in particular, remains negligible. The 1996 British Crime Survey showed that 16–29 year olds from minority ethnic groups were much less likely to have used drugs than their white counterparts; 46 per cent of white young people said they had taken drugs compared with 31 per cent of African Caribbeans, 22 per cent of Indians and 16 per cent of Pakistanis/Bangladeshis (Ramsay and Spiller,

1997). The survey results also show that, whilst women are less likely than men to use drugs, white and African-Caribbean women (26 per cent) are significantly more likely to do so than Asian women (8 per cent). Cannabis was the most widely used drug followed by amphetamines across all major ethnic groups.

Whilst there is some evidence of under-utilisation of drugs services (Pearson and Patel, 1998), and attitudes towards drug use (Karlsen *et al.*, 1998; Khan *et al.*, 1998), little is known about the circumstances under which black young people may turn to drugs, or the implications of such drug use.

In a qualitative study of 132 young people (aged 12–13) in inner London secondary schools, Karlsen *et al.* (1998) found that religious and peer influences were closely associated with ethnicity. The researchers document that Bangladeshi adolescents reported higher levels of religious involvement and lower levels of substance misuse. White adolescents showed the opposite pattern, while African and African-Caribbean adolescents were found to be between the two extremes.

In a national random survey of young people aged 14–21 in England and Wales, Bowling *et al.* (1994) found that one in four whites compared to one in eight Africans and African Caribbeans, and one in 12 Asians had used and/or sold drugs in the last year. More recent writings, however, document a trend of increasing drug use amongst Asian young people (Bennetto, 2000; Barn and Sidhu, 2000; Rashid and Rashid, 2000).

It is of concern that, although the problem of substance misuse is popularly associated with some black groups, they continue to be under-represented among known populations of drug users. Pearson and Patel (1998) question this under-representation given that black groups suffer disproportionately from social exclusion in terms of poverty, unemployment, poor housing and educational disadvantage (Modood *et al.*, 1997), and in the light of the fact that research evidence has consistently pointed to a concentration of the most serious drug-related problems in areas of high deprivation and disadvantage.

The low referral and the low use of drugs services by black groups have been explained by some writers as a consequence of problems around accessibility and lack of appropriateness of service provision (Flemen, 1995; Desson, 1998). Awiah *et al.* (1992) highlighted the need for education, information, counselling and advice, both for users and their families. They also reported that young Asians were unlikely to use specialist drug services for a variety of reasons, including a perception that they were white oriented.

Some of the issues and concerns highlighted by drugs projects (Desson, 1998) to reach out to the black community include:

- an identification of community perceptions of the problems associated with drugs for individuals, their families and the community

- to establish the type of drug prevention strategies perceived to be the most appropriate and most likely to be supported locally

- to raise awareness of drug misuse and encourage community responses to the issue

- to identify appropriate methods of delivering services and support to those involved in substance misuse.

Drug services that are proving to be successful in attracting black clients appear to have paid considerable attention to the above factors. In a recent empirical study, the author found worryingly high levels of substance misuse amongst Bangladeshi young boys in East London (Barn and Sidhu, 2000). One drugs project reported that 65 per cent of the drug-using clients under the age of 18 were Bangladeshi. This is a phenomenal statistic and requires urgent attention. It's also worrying to note that the drugs of choice were Class A drugs, namely heroin and crack/cocaine. Bangladeshi boys as young as 14 were said to be addicted to heroin, quite often as a result of being introduced to the drug by an older sibling. Poor housing, over-crowding, low educational attainment and poverty were cited as causal factors by drugs workers in this area.

Research evidence into substance misuse and black young people has, by and large, identified low levels of access and utilisation of drugs services amongst black young people. Consequently, this has led to the view that black young people may use softer drugs such as cannabis, but may not be involved in heavy use of Class A drugs such as heroine and cocaine. It is important that research is conducted to explore the nature and extent of substance misuse problems amongst black young people to combat misplaced complacency that may exist in this area.

Mental health

In recent years, there has been an increasing recognition of mental health problems amongst children and young people. Research studies document that one in five children and young people experience a wide range of mental health problems. Research has made strong links between child mental heath problems and other issues of public concern such as substance misuse, juvenile crime, self-harm and eating disorders.

Whilst the identity development of black children and young people has been a concern for researchers (see Chapter 4), there is a dearth of literature exploring risk factors which may lead to mental health problems. Consequently, we know little about the prevalence of black children to suffer from mental health problems, or their qualitative experiences of services.

In a discussion about Asian people, Harris (2000) believes that, because of the complex cultural and religious diversity, epidemiological research into mental health problems and service provision has been largely problematic. In a similar vein, Bird (1996, p. 43) stated that ' a widely accepted methodology for epidemiological surveys of mental disorders of children and adolescents that can be used systematically with different cultural groups and applied in different cultural settings is yet to be developed'. Western psychiatry has been much criticised for its eurocentric tools of diagnosis and the negative impact of these on disadvantaged black groups (Burke, 1986; Fernando, 1988). Such a situation is likely to continue unless and until current methods of practice and research break out of the eurocentric straightjacket and adopt a diverse framework (Harris, 2000).

Risk factors

Socio-economic circumstances

Research evidence into mental health problems indicates the powerful and negative impact of socio-economic disadvantage including poor housing, overcrowding, low incomes, unemployment, isolation and discrimination. The Audit Commission (1999) documents that certain groups of children, and those living in certain conditions, are at greater risk of developing mental health problems than others:

- Forty per cent of children with mental health problems were found to be living with only one birth parent – either in a lone-parent family or with a step-parent in a reconstituted family, compared to about 21 per cent of the general population.

- Thirty-four per cent were living in families where the main breadwinner was unemployed.

- Twenty-seven per cent had some form of learning disabilities.

- Nineteen per cent were living with a parent with mental illness.

- Nine per cent of children were looked after by the local authority.

It is unfortunate that the Audit Commission makes no reference to the mental health needs and concerns of black young people. Given the above statistics, and our understanding and knowledge of disadvantage and discrimination experienced by black communities, it could be inferred that some black children and young people are at serious risk of developing mental health problems.

Racial abuse and racist bullying

The effects of racial abuse and racist bullying, and racial discrimination can add to the vulnerability experienced by black young people (National Children's Home, 1998). Bose (2000) highlights the distressing impact of covert discrimination felt by black young people. This includes poor expectations and negative stereotyping from teachers, being 'overlooked' in groups, and less enthusiasm from careers officers about their future plans (Wright, 1987; Bose, 2000). Issues and concerns around racist bullying have been highlighted elsewhere (Childline, 1997; National Children's Home, 1998; Barter, 1999).

Table 4 illustrates the prevalence of bullying and racial harassment felt by young people in two multi-racial London boroughs (Batra, 1988; London Borough of Newham 1988). These reports by Batra (1988) and London Borough of Newham (1988) illustrate the offensive, alienating and pervasive nature of bullying at school. As can be seen in Table 4, much of this behaviour translates into overt racial harassment.

Racial attacks and harassment of families and individuals in the community are another area of concern. Whilst there are national data sets (for example, Police Statistics and the British Crime Survey) to signify the extent of racial violence and harassment, little is known about the effects of racial harassment on people's lives (Gordon, 1989). It is important that serious attention is directed to this area as it may affect minority groups in a number of ways. Virdee (1997) identifies a range of strategies adopted by minority ethnic people who worry about racial harassment. These included 'avoiding going out at night', 'making home more secure', 'visiting shops at certain times only', 'stopping children from playing outside' and 'avoiding areas where mostly white people live'.

Table 4 Young people's experiences of racial harassment and racial bullying in two London boroughs

	Bullying		Racial harassment	
	Newham (%)	Ealing (%)	Newham (%)	Ealing (%)
Asian	43	34	16	19
Caribbean	35	53	16	27
White	34	58	8	7

Source: Luthra (1997, p. 200).

Young carers

Distress in young people may emanate from a variety of sources. Shah and Pattern (2000) highlight the isolation experienced by young carers from the Asian community. The researchers focused on the experiences of young carers in South Asian communities who were in contact with two Barnardo's young carers projects. Semi-structured interviews were carried out with 19 young carers in South Asian communities living in 13 households, to explore participants' views of various aspects of their lives.

The research study found that young carers report themselves as caring for a parent in isolation, with little practical or emotional support from other people.

Wider family members, where they live locally, provide little practical support and are seen as largely unsupportive. There was a cultural expectation by the wider family that it was the young person's duty to continue to provide care.

An important message from this research is the need for health, social care and education professionals to identify young carers from all communities and offer appropriate services.

Asian girls and mental health

The high incidence of suicide attempts among young Asian adolescent girls has been highlighted by some researchers (Merrill, 1986; Soni-Raleigh et al., 1990). In one research study, Asian young women in the age group 15–24 showed levels of completed suicide 80 per cent higher than the general rate for white women of a corresponding age (Soni-Raleigh et al., 1990). Such incidences have been explained in terms of familial pressures to conform to Asian values including 'arranged marriages' and young women's desire to fit into western society. Some research into eating disorders has also shown a small number of cases of anorexia nervosa and bulimia nervosa among Asian schoolgirls (Bhadrinath, 1990; Mumford et al., 1991).

Researchers have pointed to cultural conflicts between parents and young women as contributory to eating disorder problems.

Protective factors

Rutter *et al.* (1979) and Rutter (1985) have identified protective factors in children's responses to stress and disadvantage, highlighting their influence in modifying, ameliorating and altering a person's response to some environmental hazard that predisposes them to a maladaptive outcome. Research studies in the United States into migrants and mental health suggest that a preservation of some of the cultural traditions, rituals and ceremonies have a protective function (Warheit *et al.*, 1985; Turner, 1991).

In a qualitative study of 145 young people in Scotland, 25 of whom were of Chinese and Muslim Pakistani ethnic background, Armstrong *et al.* (2000) found that mental health views and attitudes of the young people from black background were very similar to the mainstream sample. However, they found that, although close family relationships were important to all the young people interviewed, young people from Muslim/Pakistani backgrounds identified the family as particularly important sources of support.

Future research needs to focus on the prevalence of mental health problems amongst different groups of black young people and explore their qualitative experiences. Moreover, an identification of protective factors such as cultural traditions, rituals and ceremonies, links with country of origin, and religious beliefs and practices requires empirical consideration. It is vital, therefore, that traditional methods of research into mental health are adapted to incorporate cultural and religious diversity of different minority ethnic groups.

Juvenile justice

Black groups comprise about 5 per cent of the total British population. It is of concern that official statistics and research studies over the last few decades have shown a disproportionate number of some minority groups, notably African Caribbean, in the criminal justice system. Concern has also been expressed about Asian youth and criminal activity including violence, usually inter-ethnic/religious, and drugs (Pring, 1996; Trivedi, 1997; Hopkins, 1999; Ghalab, forthcoming). The recent civil disturbances in northern English towns such as Oldham, Bradford, Leeds and Burnley involving white and Asian youths signify deep racial divisions between the two communities, and will no doubt further serve to racialise Asian youth and criminality (Bodi, 2001).

About 1 per cent of the general population is African Caribbean. In 1990, 11 per cent of the male sentenced prisoners and 24 per cent of female sentenced prisoners were African Caribbean (Home Office, 1992). African-Caribbean people have been shown to be less likely to be cautioned than their white counterparts, less likely to have a probation report presented on their behalf and less likely to receive a probation order (Moxon, 1988; Hudson, 1989; Walker, 1989). Also, it seems that insisting on trial by jury means that a higher proportion of black defendants are tried at crown court, with a greater likelihood of a custodial sentence (Moxon, 1988; Walker, 1989), and that sentences are longer if the guilty plea discount is not applicable (Hood, 1992). Brown and Hullin (1992) documented that proportionately more black than white defendants were committed for trial at the crown court as a result of recommendations by the Crown Prosecution Service rather than not guilty pleading.

Young offenders from all minority ethnic groups tend to serve longer sentences than white young offenders (Home Office, 1997). In June 1996, the proportion of white young offenders serving sentences of over 18 months was 71 per cent compared with 87 per cent Africans/Caribbeans, 79 per cent South Asians, and 75 per cent Chinese and other groups.

In relation to black young people and cautions, there is research evidence to show that African-Caribbean juveniles are less likely than whites to be cautioned; a white juvenile with previous convictions may be more than four times more likely to receive a caution than a black juvenile in similar circumstances (Landau and Nathan, 1983). It seems that, if cautions are more readily given to young people who live with both parents and whose parents are in employment (Landau and Nathan, 1983), then it is less likely that African-Caribbean young people will be dealt with in this way. African-Caribbean youngsters are more likely to come from a lone-parent family (47 per cent), compared to white youngsters (17 per cent). Other research evidence shows that only half as many young African Caribbeans as whites admitted the offence of which they were accused (Commission for Racial Equality, 1992). Since a caution can only be given following an admission of guilt, it would seem that this may be part of the explanation. Dholakia and Sumner (1993) suggest that perhaps black young people are being treated as suspects for offences which they did not commit.

Research evidence into 'race' and crime suggests racial prejudice on the part of the police, probation officers, magistrates and judges, and prison administrators (Whitehouse, 1983; National Association for the Care and Resettlement of Offenders, 1989; Hudson, 1993). Qualitative studies into court reports have shown that black defendants are discussed in negative terms which make custodial sentences more rather than less probable (Whitehouse, 1983). Reports on black defendants were found to contain references to migration, to cultural traditions of child-rearing outside marriage and to black people having children with several partners. Hudson (1993) argues that, while some such references

57

might be intended to provide mitigation, they have the opposite effect since black family patterns do not match the ideals of the largely white, middle-aged, middle-class magistracy and judiciary. Thus, a magistrate or a judge may feel that the risk of reoffending is too high to justify a community penalty.

Concern about racism and policing, recently profiled by the Macpherson Report (1999), has been highlighted since 1970 when Gus John wrote his influential study of Handsworth called *Race in the Inner City* and John Lambert published a study of *Crime, Police and Race Relations.* Both studies attracted attention because they came out at a time when concern was being expressed about relations between the black community and policing, and the involvement of young black people in crime. Media coverage at the time talked of the growing tensions between the police and black communities, and 1969–70 saw a number of minor street confrontations with the police in areas such as Notting Hill.

Solomos (1993) documents that evidence from black communities across the country highlighted three important issues. These included complaints by black young people that they were being categorised as a problem group by the police, and therefore more likely to be questioned or arrested; allegations that the police used excessive physical force in their dealings with black suspects; and that such attitudes and forms of behaviour by the police were creating deep divisions between the police and the black community. Solomos (1993) believes that the Select Committee on Race Relations and Immigration, and media coverage in the early 1970s were the beginnings of the criminalisation of African-Caribbean young people and the racialisation of street crimes such as mugging.

Hall *et al.* (1978) documented that the street crime of mugging became associated with black youth because they were seen as the social group which suffered the most direct impact of the cycle of poverty, unemployment and social alienation. Moreover, they were perceived to come from a 'weak' culture, and had high levels of social problems such as broken families and lack of achievement in schools. Hall *et al.* believe that, even in areas where young black people were a small minority of the total youth population, the issue of crime on the streets became intimately tied with the category of black youth. It would appear that the inner-city disturbances of the early- and mid-1980s further added to the image of young black people as intimately involved in street crime and in confrontations with the police.

Despite the efforts made over the last two decades, in particular, to tackle the prevalence of racial discrimination in the criminal justice system, racism still persists. The Macpherson Report (1999) has been the most recent in a series of government inquiries into a range of social issues to document the prevalence of institutional racism.

In terms of a research understanding of the issues and concerns, it would appear that, with the exception of a few academic empirical research studies, little is actually known about the qualitative experiences of black young people in the criminal justice system. A reliance on government statistics allows the theorisation of criminal activity, but it adds little to our understanding of the experiences of young people involved with the police, the courts, the probation and the prison service. Qualitative research in these areas would enable us to understand the complexity of factors, and the perceived impact of policy and practice initiatives.

4 RACIAL AND CULTURAL IDENTITY

The notion and development of a black identity has become the subject of much study in modern western societies. The historical domination of black people by white European people over the last 400 years and the associated racial superiority/inferiority theories have created a racial paradigm which continues to be influential. In any discussion about identity, there are parallel debates around racial assimilation, integration and separation. Much emphasis is placed on the ways in which black communities adopt and adapt to the mainstream influences of their environment, and the retention of their own cultural/religious and social mores. Arguments have centred around levels of acculturation/adaptation to host society, impact of migration, religion, ethnicity and racism in society.

The issue of identity for children from a minority ethnic background living in a country such as Britain is particularly poignant. The negotiation and assertion of a black identity becomes a daily struggle in a country which is largely incongruous with one's own self-image. Britain's credentials as a predominantly white, Christian country with a history of slavery and colonialism, and continuing racial disadvantage and discrimination play a significant role.

Postmodern thinking about the changing nature of identity and its fluidity may be relevant (Gilroy, 1987, 2000; Modood *et al.*, 1994; Ghuman, 1997); however, Britain is far from a melting-pot situation where 'race' is a non-issue. Whilst social class, gender and other variables play an important role, racial and cultural identity is still the over-riding consideration for the majority and minority populations (Mama, 1995; Modood *et al.*, 1997). Such racial and cultural importance is echoed by the black British-Caribbean journalist Trevor Phillips in an article on ethnic diversity in London:

> "The loss of identity is not an option for young Londoners – my children's generation have no doubts about their heritage and they won't give it up easily."
>
> (Phillips, 2000, p. 22)

Over the last 50 years, there has been an increasing interest in the identity development of black children. The lack of similar interest in white children signifies an unspoken 'norm' about the ways in which white children's identity develops in multi-racial societies. Thus, the focus on black children as the objects of study has led to a situation where the identity formation of white young people is perceived as unproblematic, and that of minority young people as rife with concern and worry. Recent focus on white ethnicity and young people suggests that serious consideration needs to be given to the ways in which white young people conceptualise and locate themselves in a racially ordered society (Rutherford, 1997; Nayak, 1999).

Theorisation of identity

The notion of identity is contested and complex. The various strands of 'race', ethnicity, social class, religion, gender and sexuality are arguably the key determining influences.

Thomas (1986, p. 372) makes a distinction between cultural and ethnic identity, and also employs another categorisation of racial identity. He defines these as follows:

- *Ethnic self-identity*: this is the label a person prefers to adopt, for example, mixed-parentage, British Caribbean, etc.

- *Ascribed ethnic identity*: this is the label others give to a person, for example, black.

- *Cultural identity*: this is the degree to which a person is familiar with and prefers a particular life style.

- *Racial identity*: this is based on physical appearance, for example, skin colour.

- *Nationality*: this is based on country of birth or citizenship; and descent – based on ethnicity of parents.

Whilst the above categorisations may be useful, it is important to highlight the complexity of terms such as 'ethnic' and 'racial' identity. There are also clearly issues around self-identity and ascribed identity. For example, an individual may self-identify their ethnicity as mixed parentage; however, others may ascribe a particular ethnic identity on to them such as black, or vice versa.

The terms 'racial' and 'ethnic' identity are often used interchangeably. However, they are not identical, although there may be some overlap. Ethnic identity refers to 'one's sense of belonging to an ethnic group and the part of one's thinking, perception, feelings, and behaviour that is due to ethnic group membership' (Phinney and Rosenthal, 1992, p. 147). An ethnic group 'refers to people who share a common history, language, religion, and culture' (Tizard and Phoenix, 1993, p. 4). Racial identity refers to a 'sense of group or collective identity based on one's perception that he or she shares a common racial heritage with a particular group' (Helms, 1990, p. 50). As with ethnic identity, a sense of belonging is a crucial part of the concept of racial identity. The main difference is that the critical attributes examined when one is talking about racial identity are those to do with 'race' rather than ethnicity. Racial identity theories do not suppose that racial groups are 'biologically distinct, but rather suppose that they have endured different conditions of domination or oppression' (Helms, 1990, p. 181). Membership of these groups is determined by 'socially defined inclusion criteria (for example, skin colour) that are commonly (mistakenly) considered to be racial in nature' (Helms, 1990, p. 181).

Whilst the major arguments centre around 'ethnic' and 'racial identity', some writers have employed other terms such as cultural identity. For example, Keats (1997, p. 87) describes cultural identity as 'that component of the concept of the self which is concerned with one's sense of embeddedness in one's family past, present and future and one's place in the wider cultural milieu'. In broad terms, Keats (1997) locates cultural identity within one's ethnic background, identifies a number of psychological attributes including 'affective', 'perceptual' and 'cognitive', and argues that one's perception of oneself is linked to one's level of self-esteem.

The debate and interest in the identity formation of black young people is most hotly contested in the context of substitute family placements (Divine, 1983; Gill and Jackson, 1983; Small, 1984; Maxime, 1993; Owusu-Bempah, 1994; Robinson, 1995). Outside the social work arena, there is much discussion about the ways in which black minority ethnic young people construct their identity, and how it may or may not differ from their parents. Moreover, the impact of majority culture, globalisation and the relative contribution of parenting behaviour have been highlighted (Gilroy, 1987; Tizard and Phoenix, 1993; Ghuman, 1997). Attention is also focused on the effects of migration, 'westernisation'/ acculturation, differing and conflicting values between parents and young people, and the impact of institutionalised and individual racism (Barn and Sidhu, 2000).

Gilroy argues that the tendency to reify racial identity as of unique importance to the individual 'reduces the complexity of self-image and personality formation in the Black child to the single issue of race/colour' (1987, p. 66). This can result in the neglect of other important social identities, such as gender and social class (see Mama, 1995). The concept of racialisation indicates the social construction of 'race' as a significant dimension in contemporary identities. But it cannot be an inclusive personal identity. Other variables, such as gender, age, class, sexual preference and nationality, are some of the other important social identities. Modood *et al.* (1994) argue that, in Britain, the last few years have seen the emergence of 'a plurality of identities, of competition between identities'. Thus, while some groups assert a racial identity based on the experience of racism, others choose to emphasise their family origins and country of origin, and others group around a caste or a religious sect.

The transracial adoption literature highlights problems and concerns around black children and identity. In the third longitudinal study into transracial adoptions in Britain, Gill and Jackson (1983) documented that there was little evidence of a positive sense of racial identity; that is, the majority of the children in the study 'perceived themselves to be White in all but skin colour' (Gill and Jackson 1983, p. 81). Gill and Jackson attributed this to the fact that the adoptive families had raised these children within a 'melting-pot' framework where highlighting racial and ethnic differences was considered inappropriate. The lack of contact with people from their own racial and cultural background was also a significant factor in the socialisation of these children. Gill and Jackson pointed out that, in spite of the racial and ethnic identity problems, the transracially adopted children were making good progress at school and seemed to be well adjusted in their families and neighbourhood.

The Gill and Jackson study and other research evidence from the USA (Simon and Alstein, 1981; McRoy *et al.*, 1982; Simon and Alstein, 1992) raise important questions about racial and ethnic identity, and its interrelated components around self-esteem and self-concept. Tizard and Phoenix (1989) make a distinction between racial identity and self-concept as two distinctly independent variables. They believe that it is possible for black children to have negative feelings about their racial identity and yet have a positive self-concept. Nick Banks questions this distinction. He argues that 'an integrated personality involves one having a stable concept of self as an individual as well as a group (Black) identity', whereby 'Black identity becomes an extension and indeed is part of the child's self-identity' (Banks, 1992, p. 21). Banks (1992) suggests that the eurocentric psychological perspectives require a significant perceptual shift to even begin to be relevant to considering the identity formation of black children and adolescents.

Clark and Clark's (1940, 1947, 1950) seminal work into racial identification, preference and identity in the 1940s and 1950s paved the way for numerous other studies in several countries around the world including Britain (Stevenson and Stewart, 1958; Vaughan, 1964; Gregor and MacPherson, 1966; Milner, 1975; Davey and Mullin, 1980). The Clarks' major finding of three to seven year olds was that black children showed preference for white skin colour, misidentified themselves as white and attributed positive characteristics to the colour white and negative to the colour black. In the racially segregated United States of the 1950s, such findings played a significant role, for example, in the *Brown* v. *Board of Education* case which led to school desegregation. It was held that such findings indicate that school segregation reinforced black children's feelings of inferiority causing low self-esteem and self-image.

Using the Clark and Clark methodological tools, Milner (1975) in a British study of 300 children between the ages of five and eight suggested that African-Caribbean and Asian children showed a preference for the white majority group and demonstrated a tendency to devalue their own group.

Research studies highlighting black self-hatred have theorised that living in a racist white society, where black people are perceived and treated as inferior leading to social and economic disadvantage and discrimination, results in black people developing a low self-image and low self-esteem. Such thinking has been challenged in the last few decades (Taylor, 1976; Barnes, 1981; Owusu-Bempah, 1994). The validity of a model that treats black people as a homogenous mass has been questioned. Also, it has been argued that there are positive counter-challenges to widespread societal racism in the form of the black family, institutions and community. These can recognise the negative messages from society, and serve to counter them with positive aspects of black family life and history.

However, Luthra (1997) has argued that some black families may not be able to transmit ethnic and cultural values within a historical context because of their lack of education:

"While parents can help in terms of passing on folk culture, their own lack of education in many cases does not help the much-needed transmission of values in a rational framework."
(Luthra, 1997, p. 33)

Similarly, Bose (2000) has identified a lack of formal cultural input in Bangladeshi families. She argues that the rural Sylhet background of Bangladeshis in East London means that they are only fluent in the Bengali dialect of Sylheti and most are lacking in English language skills. Such linguistic disadvantage on two levels results in Bangladeshi parents not being able to engage with children in English or Bengali. Bose draws an implication from this for children's understanding and knowledge of Bengali history:

> "Sylheti uses the script for standard Bengali, which is unfamiliar to most parents, who therefore cannot teach written Bengali to their children. This has implications for their children's access to the knowledge of Bengali history, stories and cultural heroes."
>
> (Bose, 2000, p. 55)

Luthra (1997) and Bose (2000) question the capability of some black families to equip black children by arguing that they are not able to transmit cultural values because of their own lack of education. Both authors signify an important class and education dimension, and operate on the assumption that there is a consensual framework around the process of socialisation and the transmission of culture. Whilst it may be useful and interesting to observe similarities and differences in parental strengths and limitations within and between different socio-economic groups in both the majority and the black communities, it would be too simplistic and parochial to draw correlations between levels of education, parenting and the transmission of cultural values.

Research literature has documented the likelihood of some black young people, most notably African Caribbean and those of mixed Caribbean/white parentage, and South Asian young women, to be coming to the attention of statutory services (Ahmed, 1981; Barn *et al.*, 1997). It would be too naive to suggest that the young person has such a poorly developed self-image because of parental lack of education and ethnic socialisation that they rebel leading to the involvement of the police, the school and the social services. Whilst there are issues around general family conflict and reconciliation, it is possible that class background, and their own limited understanding of a cultural and historical framework pertaining to their own ethnic group, leaves some parents without the necessary tools to counter the negative racist influences in society. Moreover, the eurocentricity of the British education system, poverty, unemployment, poor housing and ill health require serious consideration. Also, the role of the wider society and its institutions in understanding the difficulties encountered by black young people in developing a positive self-image in an environment which does little to incorporate racial diversity actively and positively must be highlighted. Ethnic and religious diversity cannot become part of the general fabric of society as long as it is exoticised and ghettoised as alien. For black young people to feel part of British society, their own ethnic background needs to be positively valued.

Some authors have argued that the social and economic context in which children find themselves is also highly significant in shaping children's identities. For example, studies in the last 20 years in both Britain and the USA have documented high rates of black preference amongst black children (Clark, 1982; Farrell and Olson, 1983; Milner, 1983; Davey, 1987). Such a trend has been explained as having arisen from the 1960s' 'black consciousness movement'. In the British context, the emergence of Bhangra music and more recently the East/West fusions (Ackland, 1989; Sharma *et al.*, 1996); and the music influences of the Caribbean and black America have led to a unique consciousness amongst Asian and African-Caribbean youth (Gilroy, 1987). Such consciousness helps to generate a collective social identity which serves to counter negative racist messages of white society. Such an identity which is eclectic and multifaceted in nature is the new postmodern phenomenon described by writers to encompass the global influences from within the diasporas.

Ghuman and Kamath (1993, p. 7) found that, whilst black young people are beginning to form new and more culturally diverse identities than their parents, 'this does not change the fact that they continue to suffer racial abuse both in and out of school and have mixed feelings about whether they belong here'. In making recommendations for the education of young people, Ghuman (1997) stresses the importance for schools of incorporating issues to do with language and culture of origin in the curriculum and argues that such an approach would carry implications for a healthier and a culturally diverse society. In a study of Asian university students, Kumari (1999) has also argued that, because of its monolithic and eurocentric nature, the British education system is failing to adequately equip minority ethnic young people to 'make informed choices about cultural values and practices'.

This chapter has shown that there are many and complex facets to the identity formation of black young people. The role of the black family is paramount in this. However, the contribution of other agencies such as schools, the media, the courts, and health and social services is also highly significant. The social and economic changes in society, the globalisation of the world, increasing and easy access to a range of information within the diasporic framework are all contributing to new and diverse identities in which black young people are breaking down barriers. Amidst such developments, it is possible that the self-hatred theories of the mid-twentieth century are beginning to have less relevance today.

The focus of future research in this area should be to inform policy and provision. Comparative studies of black and white young people around transition to adulthood, relationships with parents and wider society are likely to be much more meaningful for a racially and culturally diverse society than a parochial focus on black young people in a vacuum.

5 CONCLUSION

This review has explored a range of areas in which minority ethnic young people may find themselves at particular risk and on the margins of society. The complexity of the situation of these young people in Britain needs to be understood in the context of their parents' migration experience, socio-economic circumstances, racial discrimination and disadvantage, and racism.

The widespread diversity between ethnic groups racially, and culturally and in their experiences of British institutions is now beginning to be recognised at policy level. Although racial inequality in a range of areas including housing, employment, education, health and social services has been documented over the last 40 years, the differential experiences of minority ethnic groups are now beginning to highlight important needs and concerns. Racial inequality continues to impact the life chances of black young people. It is crucial that there is an adequate conceptualisation of the areas of risk and vulnerability for different groups and that such conceptualisation is able to begin to influence policy and provision to reduce disadvantage and discrimination.

The following areas are highlighted as possible future targets for researchers, funding bodies and policy makers.

Young people and the personal social services

Although our knowledge base has improved in some areas – for example, admission rates of entry into care, and foster and residential placements – there is still a great dearth of research literature in many other areas. More focused research is required which can provide specific answers, but which can also place the totality of the minority experience within a wider framework. Thus, at times, it may be useful to conduct research into specific ethnic groupings where our understanding and knowledge base is particularly lacking. Overall, our interests as a nation are more likely to be served if all future research studies adopt a diversity approach. There is a real need to move away from 'tokenistic' and 'afterthought' models of research which pay lip service to the idea of a multi-racial society and add virtually nothing to our understanding. Such approaches do more damage than good as generalisations are made about minority groups based on small and unrepresentative samples.

Child protection

Research in the area of child protection has identified some issues around referral, and assessment of minority ethnic young people. The importance of well-trained and qualified interpreters in the process of assessment has also been highlighted. To a large extent, research in this area remains patchy. However, it has raised important questions about child rearing and child punishment within different communities, and the ways in which helping agencies conceptualise minority ethnic cultures. Further research is needed to address the gaps identified. Moreover, it is important that studies contextualise minority ethnic families' experiences within a holistic and structural framework, and that adequate account is taken of the four elements included in the 1989 Children Act, sec. 22(5)(c) – namely, 'race', culture, religion and language.

Some questions which need to be addressed include the following:

- What is the experience of minority ethnic families following child protection referrals to the social services?

- How are families involved in child protection assessment and registration?

- What support is given to families pre/post registration?

- What support is given to non-English-speaking families?

- What are minority families' views about child punishment, child-rearing, etc.?

- How do practitioners build 'race' and ethnicity into the assessment process?

- What is the impact of racism/racial harassment/racial bullying on black families and children?

- What are the qualitative experiences of families and young people in cases of child sexual abuse? In what ways does the non-offending parent become involved to protect the abused young person?

Children looked after

Our understanding of the patterns of entry into care and placements of minority ethnic young people has improved over the last couple of decades. For instance, we know that African-

Caribbean and mixed-parentage young people are more likely to be in the care system than Asian young people. The pattern of referral of Asian young women to the social services has also been highlighted. The impact of social and economic disadvantage and discrimination in the form of poor housing, unemployment and poverty on family life has been documented. It has also been suggested that the lack of adequate preventive work with black families and the conscious or unconscious racist professional ideologies may militate against families, and may increase the chances of black young people entering care.

Further research is needed to explore the experiences of minority ethnic families, and to document empirical indicators which increase or reduce the chances of minority ethnic young people entering care.

- Under what circumstances do minority ethnic children and young people enter the care system?

- What are the relative experiences of young people, their families and practitioners about the admission process?

- What is the nature and extent of family support and preventative work offered to minority ethnic families?

- What are the measurable outcomes of preventive work carried out with minority ethnic families and young people? How effective is such work?

Fostering and adoption

Research evidence into the fostering and adoption of minority ethnic young people has improved considerably over the last decade or so, but remains limited in many ways. Although there is a need for more holistic and sophisticated assessments of placement to avoid simplistic racial matching, we know that some young people (notably African Caribbean, and Asian) in inner-city areas have a good chance of being placed in foster families that reflect their own racial and cultural background. Evidence into the placement needs of mixed-parentage young people has demonstrated the complexity of racial matching. There is a lack of good evidence about organisational policies and practices, and the relative contributions of carers and young people.

Some important questions that need to be addressed include the following:

- In what ways do social care organisational policies and strategies influence practice and provision in foster care arrangements for minority ethnic children?

- How do social care agencies attempt to recruit suitable foster and adoptive carers for minority ethnic children?

- What factors help or hinder the adoption of minority ethnic young people?

- What are the relative experiences of minority ethnic young people in black and white substitute families?

- How do black and white substitute carers attempt to provide good substitute care for minority ethnic young people?

- What are the risk and protective factors in substitute placements? What are the experiences of different ethnic groups?

- What are the stabilising influences in long-term foster care and in adoptive placements of minority ethnic young people?

Residential care

Although the number of young people in residential care has fallen steadily over the last few decades, the situation of minority ethnic young people is not clear. Given the continual difficulties experienced by some agencies in finding appropriate family placements for minority ethnic young people, it is feasible that residential care is still a viable option. Previous research has documented the lack of staff competence to deal with racial tensions within homes and has pointed to the eurocentric ethos of such institutions, which are often found in rural areas outside the communities. More recent studies have shown the positive ways in which black young people can be empowered by making institutional changes including the employment of black staff, use of external mentors, and a valuing of racial and cultural diversity.

Some areas of exploration include:

- a profile of minority ethnic young people who are placed in residential care and factors which result in such placements

- the experiences of minority ethnic young people in residential care, from the perspective of young people and care staff

- the ways in which social care agencies deal with diversity and racial discrimination in residential homes.

Care leavers

Given the documented high representation of minority ethnic young people in the care system and the lengthy periods spent in care, it is ironic that little is actually known about their care-leaving experiences. Although we can deduce from mainstream research about the likelihood of minority ethnic young care leavers to be represented in the indices of social exclusion of homelessness, poor educational attainment and unemployment, we lack good research evidence which can tell us about risk and vulnerability. Previous research has highlighted the lack of racial and cultural input, and the problems of isolation and loneliness; it is important to conduct further research in these areas to ascertain the experiences of young people and to find ways in which policy and practice could be developed to combat such problems.

Some research questions include the following:

- In what ways do social care agencies incorporate 'race' and ethnicity into their work in preparing minority ethnic young people to cope with life after care?

- What are the post-care experiences of black and white young people in education, employment, training, housing and health, and social welfare?

Other vulnerable groups

Whilst we have some understanding of minority ethnic young people in areas such as education and juvenile justice, there are many gaps in our understanding in these and several other areas such as housing and homelessness, substance misuse and mental health. It is crucial that we address these gaps to enhance the life chances of vulnerable young people.

Education, employment and training

Research evidence over the last few decades has documented differential patterns between ethnic groups in educational attainment, and employment and training opportunities. Some groups (namely African Caribbean, Pakistani and Bangladeshi) have fared worst in all of these areas. It is important that research moves beyond the quantitative phase to offer an analysis of the significant factors around 'race', class and gender to begin to make an impact on young people's lives. Qualitative research into why some groups do better than others, the role of the education system in incorporating diversity, an evaluation of innovative practices in combating lower educational attainment and school exclusion, and the factors which result in differential patterns in employment and training require urgent attention.

Some areas of focus include the following:

- What factors contribute to the educational attainment of minority ethnic young people?

- How can we explain attainment disparities between different minority ethnic groups?

- How does the education system (teachers, governors, ethos, curriculum) affect the educational chances of minority ethnic groups?

- How useful and effective is the practice of ethnic monitoring and tracking of pupil attainment?

- What factors lead to the school exclusion of minority ethnic young people?

- What are the relative merits/de-merits of community mentoring schemes? How effective are such ventures?

- What factors contribute to choices made by minority ethnic young people to stay on at school, or leave school?

- What are the qualitative experiences of minority ethnic young people in the labour market?

Homelessness

There is some research evidence to show the differential patterns of homelessness and help-seeking behaviour experienced by different ethnic groups. We know that African-Caribbean young people are more likely to be homeless than Africans and Asians, and that Africans are more likely to be homeless than Asians. Because of the small sample size of Asians in research studies, we do not know whether there are differences between Indians, Pakistanis and Bangladeshis. Research evidence tells us that minority ethnic young people are more likely to stay with friends than white young people and are less likely to sleep on the street. It is of concern that, although minority ethnic young people are found to be less likely than whites to call on the help of statutory agencies, they still constitute 50 per cent of those who come to the attention of homelessness agencies. The representation of school excludees and those from the care system amongst the homeless population is a worrying trend.

Some areas of exploration include the following:

- Under what circumstances do minority ethnic young people become homeless?

- What are the qualitative experiences of minority ethnic young people in their use and access of services?

- How do helping agencies attempt to reach and support minority ethnic young people?

Substance misuse

Research evidence into substance misuse amongst minority ethnic young people remains patchy. There is some evidence to suggest lower levels of drug use amongst minority ethnic young people than white young people, and lower levels of access and utilisation of drugs services. Consequently, such research has reinforced the image of the drug user as white, young and male, and has led to the perception that black young people may use softer drugs such as cannabis, but may not be involved in heavy drug use. Given recent research evidence pointing to heavy drug use amongst Bangladeshi youth, it is important that further research is conducted to explore the nature and extent of substance misuse problems amongst minority ethnic young people to combat previously held myths and to begin to address the needs and concerns of all drug users.

Some areas of consideration include the following:

- What are the nature and extent of substance misuse problems amongst minority ethnic young people?

- What factors help/hinder minority ethnic young people to access and make use of drugs services?

- How do drugs agencies attempt to address the needs and concerns of minority ethnic young people?

Mental health

Little is known about the prevalence of minority ethnic children to suffer from mental health problems, or their qualitative experiences of services. This is a serious omission given the disadvantage and discrimination experienced by minority ethnic young people in a range of areas. Whilst research has focused on adult users of mental health services from minority communities, our understanding about the situation of young people in these communities remains limited. The research community needs to focus its efforts on rates of prevalence of mental health problems – nature, use and access of services, and an understanding of risk and protective factors in promoting mental well-being.

Research questions should include the following:

- What are the nature and extent of mental health problems experienced by minority ethnic young people?

- What are the risk and protective factors in mental well-being for minority ethnic young people?

- How do racial abuse and racist bullying affect the mental well-being of minority ethnic young people?

- What are the qualitative experiences of minority ethnic young people's access and use of mental health services?

- How do mental health services attempt to integrate 'race' and ethnicity into their policies, practice and provision?

Juvenile justice

In terms of a research understanding of the issues and concerns, it would appear that, with the exception of a few academic empirical research studies, little is actually known about the qualitative experiences of black young people in the criminal justice system. A reliance on government statistics allows the theorisation of criminal activity, but it adds little to our understanding of the experiences of young people involved with the police, the courts, the probation and the prison service. Qualitative research in these areas would enable us to understand the complexity of factors, and the perceived impact of policy and practice initiatives.

Some areas of consideration include the following:

- What are the qualitative experiences of minority ethnic young people in the juvenile justice system (police, probation officers, social workers, magistrates/judges, prison officers)?

- What factors contribute to a greater likelihood of custodial sentences for minority ethnic young people than for white young people?

- What is the nature and extent of anti-racist training, and other anti-racist initiatives within the juvenile justice system? How effective are these in ensuring racial justice?

Identity

Racial and ethnic identity in western multi-racial and multi-cultural societies continues to occupy the minds of social scientists, journalists and other writers. Much of the focus is on the ways in which minorities conceptualise and develop their racial and ethnic identity, and little attention is paid to the identity formation of white young people.

The focus of future research in this area should be to inform policy and provision. Comparative studies of black and white young people around transition to adulthood, relationships with parents and wider society are likely to be much more meaningful for a racially and cultural diverse society than a parochial focus on black young people in a vacuum.

- How do black and white young people conceptualise their ethnic identity?

- What are the determining influences on young people's sense of their ethnic identity?

- How does ethnicity influence transition to adulthood, relationships with parents and wider society?

This review has outlined the context in which some black young people present their vulnerability. It is important that there is a partnership between research, policy and practice. Whilst research can highlight areas of concern, and how these may be changing, policy makers and practitioners can target groups with appropriate help and intervention. Research into the effectiveness of intervention with minority groups is chronically under-developed. This is an important area in which the academic and the practice community need to get together in the interests of minority ethnic families and children.

In terms of policy development, it has to be said that, in the absence of local and national statistics, agencies are ill-equipped to plan and deliver appropriate services. In our 1997 study, *Acting on Principle* (Barn *et al.*, 1997), we highlighted the need for appropriate management information systems. It is good to learn that the Department of Health will be collating information on ethnic origin of children looked after (Department of Health, 2000). In the field of education, data on ethnic monitoring and individual pupil attainment will be available from 2001. It is important to state that collation of information is not an end in itself. Appropriate action, and service delivery are crucial. Management information systems have to be accountable, and tied into appropriate targets and action.

The availability of national and local data will reduce the need for certain number-crunching research. It is important that qualitative research is carried out to illustrate the quantitative patterns reflected in government statistics. Official statistics will need to be treated with caution and in a critical light.

There is a considerable body of research evidence which highlights the dangers of accumulated deprivation and disadvantage. The life chances of black young people are affected by a range of variables leading to their high representation in statistics around children looked after, homelessness, the juvenile justice system and unemployment. It is vital that the potential long-term costs to society of these vulnerable young people are recognised and avoided, and appropriate action is taken to ameliorate their situation. Action of a preventative nature needs to be led by central government through local agencies to provide help and assistance to those in need. Future research needs to facilitate these efforts by focusing on resilience as well as on risk and vulnerability, and by evaluating the efficacy of policy initiatives and provisions.

NOTE

Chapter 1

1   The term minority ethnic is employed here to refer to young people of African and Asian (including Chinese) descent. Specific mention is made of particular religious and cultural groupings from within these groups to highlight differential experiences in British society.

BIBLIOGRAPHY

Abrahams, C. and Mungall, R. (1992) *Runaways: Exploding the Myths*. London: NCH

Ackland, T. (1989) 'Integration and segregation in an Asian community', *New Community*, Vol. 15

Ahmad, S. (1996) 'The status of women and fertility: a case study of Pakistani women in Rochdale', MPhil. dissertation, Sociology Department, Lancaster University

Ahmad, S. (1998) 'Gender roles and fertility: a comparative analysis of women from Britain and Pakistan', PhD dissertation, Sociology Department, Lancaster University

Ahmed, S. (1981) 'Asian girls and culture conflict', in J. Cheetham *et al.* (eds) *Social and Community Work in a Multiracial Society*. London: Harper and Row

Ahmed, S. *et al.* (eds) (1986) *Social Work with Black families and Children*. London: Batsford

Amenta Marketing (1997) *The Black Child Report*. London: Amenta Marketing

Anderson, I. (1993) *Single Homeless People*. London: Department of the Environment/The Stationery Office

Anthias, F. and Yuval-Davis, N. (1992) *Racialised Boundaries: Race, Nation, Gender, Colour, Class and the Anti-Racist Struggle*. London: Routledge

Anwar, M. (1979) *The Myth of Return: Pakistanis in Britain*. London: Heinemann

Anwar, M. (1998) *Between Cultures: Continuity and Change in the Lives of Young Asians*. London: Routledge

Armstrong, C., Hill, M. and Secker, J. (2000) 'Young people's perceptions of mental health', *Children and Society*, Vol. 14, pp. 60–72

Audit Commission (1999) *Children in Mind: Child and Adolescent Mental Health Services*. Abingdon: Bookpoint Ltd

Awiah, J. *et al.* (1992) *Race, Gender and Drug Services*. London: ISDD

Baker, J. (1999) 'Lest we forget – the children they left behind, the life experience of adults born to black GIs and British women during the Second World War', MA thesis, University of Melbourne, Australia

Ballard, R. (ed.) (1994) *Desh Pardesh, the South Asian Presence in Britain.* London: Hurst and Co.

Ballard, R. and Kalra, V.S. (1994) *The Ethnic Dimension of the 1991 Census: A Preliminary Report.* Manchester: Census Dissemination Unit, University of Manchester

Banks, N. (1992) 'Techniques for direct identity work with black children', *Adoption and Fostering*, Vol. 16, No. 3, pp. 19–25

Banks, N.J. (1996) 'Young single white mothers with black children in therapy', *Clinical Child Psychology and Psychiatry*, Vol. 1, No. 1, pp. 19–28

Barn, R. (1993) *Black Children in the Public Care System.* London: Batsford/BAAF

Barn, R. (1994) Black, White or Mixed-Race? Race and Racism in the lives of young people of mixed-parentage, Tizard, B and Phoenix, A. (1993), London: Routledge, reviewed in the Journal 'New Community', Vol. 20, No.3, pp. 554–6

Barn, R. (1998) 'Race and racism: can minority ethnic groups benefit from social work?', in J. Edwards and J.P.Revauger (eds) *Discourse on Inequality in France and Britain.* Aldergate: Ashgate

Barn, R. (1999a) 'White mothers, mixed-parentage children, and child welfare', *British Journal of Social Work*, Vol. 29, No. 2, pp. 269–84

Barn, R. (ed.) (1999b) *Working with Black Children and Adolescents in Need.* London: BAAF

Barn, R. (2000) '"Race", ethnicity and transracial adoption', in A. Treacher and I. Katz (eds) *Dynamics of Transracial Adoption.* London: JKP

Barn, R. (2001) 'Addressing the context: "race", ethnicity and child welfare', in B. Mason and A. Sawyer *Exploring the Unsaid: Risk and Creativity in Working Cross-culturally.* London: Karnac

Barn, R. and Sidhu, K. (2000) 'Health and social care: a study of Bangladeshi women in Tower Hamlets', Department of Health, unpublished

Barn, R., Sinclair, R. and Ferdinand, D. (1997) *Acting on Principle: An Examination of Race and Ethnicity in Social Services Provision for Children and Families.* London: BAAF

Barnes, E.J. (1981) 'The black community as a source of positive self-concept for black children: a theoretical perspective', in R.L. Jones (ed.) *Black Psychology*, 2nd edition. New York: Harper and Row

Barter, C. (1999) *Protecting Children from Racism and Racial Abuse: A Research Review*. London: NSPCC

Batra, S. (1988) *In the Interest of Our Children*. London: London Borough of Ealing

Batta, I. *et al.* (1981) 'Crime, social problems and Asian immigration: the Bradford experience', *International Journal of Contemporary Sociology*, Vol. 18, No. 1, pp. 135–68

Batta, I. and Mawby, R. (1981) 'Children in local authority care: a monitoring of racial differences in Bradford', *Policy and Politics*, Vol. 9, No. 2, pp. 137–49

Bebbington, A. and Miles, J. (1989) 'The background of children who enter care', *British Journal of Social Work*, Vol. 19, pp. 349–68

Bennetto, J. (2000) 'Drug addiction is surging in the Asian community', *The Independent*, 10 January

Berrington, A. (1994) 'Marriage and family formation among the white and ethnic minority populations in Britain', *Ethnic and Racial Studies*, Vol. 17, No. 3

Berthoud, R. (1999) *Young Caribbean Men and the Labour Market: A Comparison with Other Ethnic Groups*. York: York Publishing Services for the Joseph Rowntree Foundation

Bhadrinath, A. (1990) 'Anorexia nervosa in adolescents of Asian extraction', *British Journal of Psychiatry*, pp. 565–68

Bhate, S. and Bhate, S. (1996) 'Psychiatric needs of ethnic minority children', in K. Dwivedi and V.P. Varma (eds) *Meeting the Needs of Ethnic Minority Children*. London: JKP

Bhavnani, R. (1994) *Black Women in the Labour Market: A Research Review*. London: Equal Opportunities Commission

Biehal, N., Clayden, J., Stein, M. and Wade, J. (1995) *Moving on: Young People and Leaving Care Schemes*. London: HMSO

Bignall, T. and Butt, J. (2000) *Between Ambition and Achievement, Young Black Disabled People's Experiences of Independence and Independent Living*. Bristol: The Policy Press

Bird, H.R. (1996) 'Epidemiology of childhood disorders in a cross cultural context', *Journal of Child Psychology and Psychiatry* Vol. 37, No. 1, pp. 35–49

Black and In Care (1984) *Black and In Care, Conference Report*. London: Blackrose Press

(The) *Black Child Report* (1999–2000) London: People Science Intelligence Unit

Boateng, P. (1998) Speech given at an International BAAF Conference, 'Best practice in Europe for children separated from their birth parents', Bradford, 22–24 April

Bodi, F. (2001) 'Ghettos in the North', *The Guardian*, 25 June

Bose, R. (2000) 'Families in transition', in A. Lau (ed.) *South Asian Children and Adolescents in Britain*. London: Whurr Publishers

Boss, P. and Homeshaw, J. (1974) 'Coloured families and social services departments', research report, University of Leicester, School of Social Work

Bourne, J., Bridges, L. and Searle, C. (1994) *Outcaste England: How Schools Exclude Black Children*. London: Institute for Race Relations

Boushel, M. (1994) 'The protective environment of children: towards a framework for anti-oppressive, cross-cultural and cross-national understanding', *British Journal of Social Work*, Vol. 24, pp. 173–90

Boushel, M. (2000) 'What kind of people are we? "Race", anti-racism and social welfare research', *British Journal of Social Work*, Vol. 30, pp. 71–89

Boushel, M. and Sharma, G. (1995) 'Looking after black and other minority children', in S. Jackson and S. Kilroe (eds) *Looking After Children, Good Parenting: Good Outcomes*. London: HMSO

Bowling, B., Graham, J., Ross, A., Junger-Tas, J., Terlow, G.J. and Klein, M. (eds) (1994) *Delinquent Behaviour Among Young People in the Western World: First Results of an International Self-report*. Amsterdam: Kugler

Brent ACPC (1997) Personal correspondence

British Youth Council (1998) *Youth Update – Housing and Homelessness*. London: BYC

Brodie, I. and Berridge, D. (1996) *Exclusion from School: Research Themes and Issues*. Luton: University of Luton Press

Brown, C. (1984) *Black and White Britain*. London: Heinemann

Brown, I. and Hullin, R. (1992) 'A study of sentencing in the Leeds Magistrates Courts', *British Journal of Criminology*, Vol. 32, No. 1, pp. 41–53

Burke, A. (1986) 'Racism, prejudice and mental illness', in J. Cox (ed.) *Transcultural Psychiatry*. London: Croom Helm

Caesar, G. *et al*. (1994) *Black Perspectives on Services for Children and Young People in Need and their Families*. London: National Children's Bureau

Cawson, P. (1977) *Black Children in Approved Schools*. London: Department of Health and Social Security

Chand, A. (2000) 'The over-representation of black children in the child protection system: possible causes, consequences and solutions', *Child and Family Social Work*, Vol. 5, pp. 67–77

Charles, M., Stephen, R. and Thoburn, J. (1992) 'The placement of black children with permanent new families', *Adoption and Fostering*, Vol. 16, No. 3, pp. 13–19

Cheetham, J. (1981) *Social Work Services for Ethnic Minorities in Britain and the USA*. London: Department of Health and Social Security

Chestang, L. (1972) 'The dilemma of biracial adoption', in *Social Work*, Vol. 17, pp. 100–15

Childline (1997) *Bully Off*. London: Childline

Children's Society (1999) *Still Running, Children on the Street in the UK*. London: Children's Society

Clark, K. and Clark, M. (1940) 'Skin color as a factor in racial identification of Negro preschool children', *Journal of Social Psychology*, Vol. 10, pp. 591–9

Clark, K. and Clark, M. (1947) 'Racial identification and preference in Negro children', in T.M. Newcombe and E.L. Hartley (eds) *Readings in Social Psychology*. New York: Holt

Clark, K. and Clark, M. (1950) 'Emotional factors in racial identification and preference in Negro children', *Journal of Negro Children*, Vol. 19, pp. 341–50

Clark, M.L. (1982) 'Racial group concept and self-esteem in black children', *Journal of Black Psychology*, Vol. 8, pp. 75-88

Commission for Racial Equality (1978) *Multi-racial Britain: The Social Services Response*. London: CRE/ADSS

Commission for Racial Equality (1989/90) *Housing Policies in Tower Hamlets: An Investigation*. London: CRE

Commission for Racial Equality (1992) *Cautions v. Prosecutions: Ethnic Monitoring of Juveniles by Seven Police Forces*. London: CRE

Craig, T. *et al.* (1997) *Off to a Bad Start*. London: Mental Health Foundation, NCH Action for Children

Cross, M. (1989) 'Afro-Caribbeans and Asians are affected differently by British racism', *New Statesman and Society*, 7 April

Cross, M. (1994) *Ethnic Pluralism and Racial Inequality*. Utrecht: University of Utrecht

Dahya, G. (1974) 'The nature of Pakistani ethnicity in industrial cities in Britain', in A. Cohen (ed.) *Urban Ethnicity*. London: Tavistock

Daniel, W.W. (1968) *Racial discrimination in England*. Harmondsworth:Penguin

Davey, A.G. (1987) 'Insiders, outsiders and anomalies: a review of studies of identities – a reply to Olivia Foster-Carter', *New Community*, Vol. 13, No. 3, pp. 477–82

Davey, A.G. and Mullin, P.N. (1980) 'Ethnic identification and preference of British primary school children', *Journal of Child Psychology and Psychiatry*, Vol. 21, pp. 241–51

Davies, J. and Lyle, S. with Deacon, A., Law, I., Julienne, L. and Kay, H. (1996) *Homelessness Amongst Young Black and Minority Ethnic People in England*. Sociology and Social Policy Research Working Paper 15. Leeds: University of Leeds, Federation of Black Housing Organisations and CHAR

Demack, S., Drew, D. and Grimsley, M. (2000) 'Minding the gap: ethnic, gender and social class differences in attainment at 16, 1988–1995', *Race, Ethnicity and Education*, Vol. 3, No. 2, pp. 117–43

Department for Education and Employment (1997) *Permanent Exclusions from Schools in England 1995/96*. London: DfEE

Department for Education and Employment (1999) *Statistics of Education, Schools in England*. London: DfEE

Department of Health (1998) Local Authority Circular, LAC(98)20. London: DOH

Department of Health (2000) *The Children Act Report*. London: DOH

Desson, P. (1998) *Off the Wall: Perceptions of Drug Use and its Impact on the Community of Toxteth*. Liverpool: Merseyside Racial Equality Council

Dholakia, N. and Sumner, M. (1993) 'Research, policy and racial justice', in D.Cook and B. Hudson (eds) *Racism and Criminology*. London: Sage Publications

Divine, D. (1983) 'Defective, hypocritical and patronising research', *Caribbean Times*, 4 March

Drew, D., Gray, J. and Sime, N. (1992) *Against the Odds: The Education and Labour Market Experiences of Black Young People, England and Wales Youth Cohort Study*, Report R&D No. 68, Youth Cohort Series No. 19. London: Employment Department

Duncan, S. and Edwards, R. (1997) 'Lone mothers and paid work: rational or economic man or gendered moral rationalities', *Feminist Economics*, Vol. 3, p. 2

Dutt, R. and Phillips, M. (2000) 'Assessing black children in need and their families', in *Assessing Children in Need and their Families*. London: Department of Health

Dwivedi, K.N. and Varma, V.P. (1996) *Meeting the Needs of Ethnic Minority Children*. London: Jessica Kingsley

Eade, J., Vamplew, T. and Peach, C. (1996) 'The Bangladeshis: the encapsulated community', in C. Peach (ed.) *Ethnicity in the 1991 Census, Vol. 2*. London: HMSO

Eggleston, S.J. *et al.* (1986) *Education for Some: The Education and Vocational Experiences of Minority Ethnic Groups.* Stoke-on-Trent: Trentham

Erikson, E. (1968) *Identity, Youth and Crisis.* London: Faber and Faber

Evans, A. (1996) *We Don't Choose to be Homeless: Report of the National Inquiry in Preventing Youth Homelessness.* London: CHAR.

Farrell, W.C. and Olson, J.L. (1983) 'Kenneth and Mamie Clark revisited: radical identification and racial preference in dark-skinned and light-skinned black children', *Urban Education*, Vol. 18, No. 3, pp. 293–303

Fergusson, D.M., Horwood, L.R. and Lynsky, M. (1994) 'The childhood of multiple problem adolescents: a fifteen year longitudinal study', *Journal of Child Psychology and Psychiatry*, Vol. 35, pp. 1123–40

Fernando, S. (1988) *Race and Culture in Psychiatry.* London: Croom Helm

First Key (1987) *A Study of Young Black People Leaving Care.* London: CRE

Fitzherbert, K. (1967) *West Indian Children in London.* London: Bell and Sons

Flemen, K. (1995) *Making Contact: Satellite Work: An Innovative and Effective Approach to Reaching Young Drug Users.* London: Turning Point, Hungerford Drug Project

Fordham, S. (1996) *Blacked Out: Dilemmas of Race, Identity and Success at Capital High.* Chicago: University of Chicago Press

Garnett, L. (1992) *Leaving Care and After Care.* London: NCB

Ghalab, A. (forthcoming) 'British Muslim and Sikh youth violence: racism, honour and changing masculinity', PhD thesis, Royal Holloway, University of London

Ghate, D. (2000) 'Family violence and violence against children', *Children and Society*, Vol. 14, pp. 395–403

Ghuman, P.A.S. (1997) 'Assimilation or integration? A study of Asian adolescents', *Educational Research*, Vol. 39, No. 1, pp. 23–35

Ghuman, P.A.S. and Kamath, A. (1993) 'Bicultural identities: study of Asian origin children', *Bilingual Family Newsletter*, Vol. 10, No. 1, pp. 3–7

Gibbons, J. *et al.* (1995) *Operating the Child Protection System.* London: HMSO

Gill, O. and Jackson, B. (1983) *Adoption and Race.* London: Batsford/BAAF

Gillborn, D. and Gipps, C. (1996) *Recent Research on the Achievement of Ethnic Minority Pupils, Report for the Office for Standards in Education.* London: HMSO

Gillborn, D. and Mirza, H.S. (2000) *Educational Inequality, Mapping Race, Class and Gender: A Synthesis of Research Evidence.* London: Ofsted

Gilroy, P. (1987) *There Ain't No Black in the Union Jack.* London: Hutchinson

Gilroy, P. (1993) *Small Acts.* London: Serpent's Tail

Gilroy, P. (2000) *Between Camps: Nations, Cultures and the Allure of Race.* London: Allen Lane

Gordon, P. (1989) 'Hidden injuries of racism', *New Statesman and Society*, 12 May, Vol. 2, No. 49, pp. 24–5

Gregor, A.J. and McPherson, D.A. (1966) 'Racial preferences and ego-identity among white and Bantu children in the Republic of South Africa', *Genetic Psychology Monographs*, Vol. 73, pp. 217–53

Hackett, L. and Hackett, R. (1994) 'Child-rearing practices and psychiatric disorder in Gujrati and British Children', *British Journal of Social Work*, Vol. 24, pp. 191–202

Hall, S. *et al.* (1978) *Policing the Crisis: Mugging, the State, and Law and Order.* London: Macmillan

Harris, Q. (2000) 'Psychological problems in Asian Children', in A. Lau (ed.) *South Asian Children and Adolescents in Britain.* London: Whurr Publishers

Harrison, P. (1983) *Inside the Inner City: Life Under the Cutting Edge.* Harmondsworth: Penguin

Haskey, J. (1997) 'Population review: (8) The ethnic minority and overseas-born populations of Great Britain', *Population Trends*, Vol. 88, pp. 13–30

Helms, J.(1990) *Black and White Racial Identity: Theory, Research and Practice.* New York, Greenwood Press

Herrnstein, R.J. and Murray, C. (1994) *The Bell Curve, Intelligence and Class Structure in American Life.* New York: Simon and Schuster

Hoge, R.D., Andrews, D.A. and Lescheid, A.W. (1996) 'An investigation of risk and protective factors in a sample of youthful offenders', *Journal of Child Psychology and Psychiatry*, Vol. 37, pp. 319–424

Home Office (1992) *Race and the Criminal Justice System.* London: Home Office

Home Office (1997) *Prison Statistics, England and Wales 1996.* London: Home Office

Hood, R. (1992) *Race and Sentencing: A Study in the Crown Court.* Oxford: Clarendon Press

Hopkins, N. (1999) 'Met stop and search now hitting Asians', *The Guardian*, 16 December

Howe, D. and Hinings, D. (1987) 'Adopted children referred to a child and family centre', *Adoption and Fostering*, Vol. 11, No. 3, pp. 44–7

Hudson, B. (1989) 'Discrimination and disparity: the influence of race on sentencing', *New Community*, Vol. 16, No. 1, pp. 23–34

Hudson, B. (1993) 'Racism and criminology: concepts and controversies', in D. Cook and B. Hudson (eds) *Racism and Criminology.* London: Sage Publications

Humphries, C., Atkar, S. and Baldwin, N. (1999) 'Discrimination in child protection work: recurring themes in work with Asian families', *Child and Family Social Work*, Vol. 4, pp. 283–91

Hylton, C. (1997) *Family Survival Strategies, Report of a Project Initiated by Exploring Parenthood*. York: Joseph Rowntree Foundation

Ince, L. (1998) *Making It Alone: A Study of the Care Experiences of Young People*. London: British Agencies for Adoption and Fostering

Institute for the Study of Drug Dependence (1997a) Specific Intervention Area, London: ISDD

Institute for the Study of Drug Dependence (1997b) *Trends and New Developments in Drug Use*. London: ISDD

Ivaldi, G. (2000) *Surveying Adoption: A Comprehensive Analysis of Local Authority Adoptions 1998–1999 (England)*. London: BAAF

John, G. (1970) *Race in the Inner City: A Report from Handsworth*. London: Runnymede Trust

Jones, T. (1993) *Britain's Ethnic Minorities*. London: PSI

Julienne, L. (1998) 'Homelessness and young single people and minority ethnic communities', *Youth and Policy*, Vol. 59, pp. 23–37

Karlsen, S. *et al.* (1998) 'Social environment and substance misuse: a study of ethnic variations among Inner London adolescents', *Ethnicity and Health*, Vol. 3, No. 4, pp. 265–73

Karn, V. and Henderson, J. (1990) *Race, Class and Housing*. Aldershot: Gower

Kaushika, A. and Oppenheim, C. (1994) *Poverty in Black and White: Deprivation and Ethnic Minorities*. London: CPAG

Keats, D.M. (1997) *Culture and the Child, A Guide for Professionals in Child Care and Development*. Chichester: John Wiley and Sons

Khan, F. *et al.* (1998) *Ethnic Minority Drug Use in Glasgow: Part One: Comparative Attitudes and Behaviour of Young White and Asian Males*. Glasgow: Glasgow Drugs Prevention Team

Khan, V.S. (1977) 'The Pakistanis: Mirpuri villagers at home in Bradford', in J.L.Watson (ed.) *Between Two Cultures: Migrants and Minorities in Britain*. Oxford: Blackwell.

Kirton, D. (2000) *'Race', Ethnicity and Adoption*. Buckingham: Open University Press

Koh, F.M. (1988) *Oriental Children in American Homes: How do they Adjust?* East West Press

Kumari, K. (1999) 'The birth of new Asian identities', *Issues in Social Work Education*, Vol. 18, No. 2, pp. 25–30

Lakey, J. (1997) 'Neighbourhoods and housing', in T. Modood *et al. Ethnic Minorities in Britain, Diversity and Disadvantage, Fourth National Survey of Ethnic Minorities*. London: PSI

Lambert, J.R. (1970) *Crime, Police and Race Relations: A Study in Birmingham*. London: Oxford University Press

Landau, S.F. and Nathan, G. (1983) 'Selecting delinquents for cautioning in the London Metropolitan Area', *British Journal of Criminology*, Vol. 23, pp. 128–49

Lau, A. (2000) (ed.) *South Asian Children and Adolescents in Britain*. London: Whurr Publishers

London Borough of Newham (1988) *Boosting Educational Achievement, an Enquiry Report*. London: London Borough of Newham

Luthra, M. (1997) *Britain's Black Population*. Aldershot: Arena

McCulloch, J., Batta, I. and Smith, N. (1979) 'Colour as a variable in the children's section of a local authority social services department', *New Community*, Vol. 7, pp. 78–84

Macdonald, R. (ed.) (1997) *Youth, the 'Underclass' and Social Exclusion*. London: Routledge

Macpherson, W. (1999) *The Stephen Lawrence Inquiry Report*. London: The Stationery Office

McRoy, R.G., Zurcher, L.A., Lauderdale, M.L. and Anderson, R.N. (1982) 'Self-esteem and racial identity in transracial adoption', *Social Work*, Vol. 27, pp. 522–6

Maitra, B. and Miller, A. (1996) 'Children, families and therapists, clinical considerations and ethnic minority cultures', in K.N. Dwivedi and V. Prakash (eds) *Meeting the Needs of Ethnic Minority Children*. London: Jessica Kingsley

Majors, R., Gillborn, D. and Sewell, T. (1998) 'The exclusion of black children: implications for a racialised perspective', in *Multicultural Teaching*. Stoke-on-Trent: Trentham Books

Mama, A. (1995) *Beyond the Masks: Race, Gender and Subjectivity*. London: Routledge.

Multi-Agency Preventative Project (MAP) (2000) *Prevention is Better Than Cure*, 28-minute video. London: London Borough of Tower Hamlets.

Maxime, J. (1993) 'The importance of racial identity for psychological well being of black children', *Association of Child Psychology and Psychiatry Newsletter*, Vol. 15, No. 4, pp. 173–9

Mayet, G. (1993) 'Exclusions and schools', *Multicultural Education Review*, Vol. 15, pp. 7–9

Merrill, J. (1986) 'Ethnic differences in self-poisoning: a comparison of Asian and white groups', *British Journal of Psychiatry*, Vol. 148, pp. 708–12

Metcalf, H. and Forth, J. (2000) *Business Benefits of Race Equality at Work*, DfEE Research Report 177. London: DfEE

Miles, R. (1982) *Racism and Migrant Labour*. London: Routledge

Milner, D. (1975) *Children and Race*. Harmondsworth: Penguin

Milner, D. (1983) *Children and Race, Ten Years On*. London: Alan Sutton Publishing

Modood, T. (1997) 'Culture and identity', in T. Modood *et al. Ethnic Minorities in Britain, Diversity and Disadvantage*. London: PSI

Modood, T., Beishon, S. and Virdee, S. (1994) *Changing Ethnic Identities*. London: PSI

Modood, T. *et al.* (1997) *Ethnic Minorities in Britain, Diversity and Disadvantage*. London: PSI

Mosby, L. *et al.* (1999) 'Troubles in interracial talk about discipline: an examination of African American Child Rearing Narratives', *Journal of Comparative Family Studies*, Vol. 30, No. 3, pp. 489–521

Moxon, D. (1988) *Sentencing Practice in the Crown Courts*, Home Office Research Study No. 103. London: HMSO

Mumford, D.B., Whitehouse, A.M. and Platts, M. (1991) 'Sociocultural correlates of eating disorders among Asian schoolgirls in Bradford', *British Journal of Psychiatry*, Vol. 158, pp. 222–8

Murji, K. (1999) 'White lines: culture, "race" and drugs', in N. South (ed.) *Drugs: Cultures, Controls and Everyday Life*. London: Sage

Nassor, I.A.A. and Simms, A. (1996) *The New Picture of Youth Homelessness in Britain*. London: Centrepoint

National Association for the Care and Resettlement of Offenders (1989) *Race and Criminal Justice: A Way Forward, A Second Report of the NACRO Race Issues National Advisory Committee*. London: NACRO

National Children's Home (1954) 'The problem of the coloured child: the experience of the National Children's Home', *Child Care Quarterly*, Vol. 8, No. 2

National Children's Home (1998) *Bullying in Schools*. London: NCH

Nayak, A. (1999) '"White English ethnicities": Racism, Anti-racism and Student Perspectives', *Race, Ethnicity and Education*, Vol. 2, No. 2, pp. 177–202

Nazroo, J.Y. (1997) *The Health of Britain's Ethnic Minorities*. London: PSI

Newham ACPC (1998) Personal correspondence

Ofsted (1999) *Raising the Attainment of Minority Ethnic Pupils*. London: Ofsted

O'Neale, V. (2000) *Excellence Not Excuses, Inspection of Services for Ethnic Minority Children and Families*. London: DoH

OPCS (1993) *1991 Census: Ethnic Group and Country of Birth (Great Britain)*. London: OPCS

Oppenheim, C. and Harker, L. (1996) *Poverty: The Facts*, 3rd edition. London: CPAG

Owen, D. (1992–95) 1991 Census Statistical Papers 1–9. Warwick: Centre for Research in Ethnic Relations, University of Warwick/CRER

Owen, D. (1993) *Ethnic Minorities in Great Britain: Housing and Family Characteristics*, 1991 Census Statistical Paper No. 4. Warwick: Centre for Research in Ethnic Relations, University of Warwick

Owusu-Bempah, K. (1994) 'Race, self-identity and social work', *British Journal of Social Work*, Vol. 24, pp. 123–36

Owusu-Bempah, K. (1999) 'Race, culture and the child', in J.Tunstill (ed.) *Children and the State*. London: Cassell

Parsons, C. (1996) 'Permanent exclusions from schools in England in the 1990s: trends, causes and responses', *Children and Society*, Vol. 10, No. 3, pp. 177–86

Pathak, S. (2000) *Race Research for the Future, Ethnicity in Education, Training and the Labour Market*, Research Topic Paper, March. London: DfEE

Payne, J. (1996) *Education and Training for 16–18 Year Olds: Individual Paths and National Trends*. London: PSI

Peach, C. and Byron, M. (1993) 'Caribbean tenants in council housing, "race", class and gender', New Community, Vol. 19, No. 3, pp. 407–23

Pearce, K.S. (1974) 'West Indian boys in Community Home Schools', *Community Schools Gazette*, Vol. 68, Nos. 6–8

Pearson, G. and Patel, K. (1998) 'Drugs, deprivation, and ethnicity: outreach among Asian drug users in a northern English city', *Journal of Drug Issues*, Vol. 28, No. 1, pp. 199–224

Phillips, D. (1987) 'Searching for a decent home, ethnic minority progress in the post-war housing market', *New Community*, Vol. 14, Nos 1/2, pp. 105–17

Phillips, T. (2000) 'London: the multicultural city', *Life* magazine, *The Observer*, 23 April

Phinney, J.S. and Rosenthal, D. (1992) 'Ethnic identity in adolescence: process, context, and outcome', in G. Adams, T. Gullotta and R. Montemayor (eds) *Adolescent Identity Formation*. London, Sage Publications

Pinder, R. (1982) *Encountering Diversity: Observation on the Social Work Assessment of Black Children*. Occasional Paper 9. Leeds: University of Leeds, Centre for Social Work and Applied Social Studies

Pinder, R. and Shaw, M. (1974) 'Coloured children in long term care', unpublished report, University of Leicester, School of Social Work

Powis, B., Griffiths, P., Gossop, M., Lloyd, C. and Strang, J. (1998) 'Drug use and offending behaviour among young people excluded from school', *Drugs Education Policy*, Vol. 5, No. 3, pp. 245–56

Pring, J. (1996) '"Lost generation" Asians feel rejected by society', *Slough Observer*, 23 February

Pritchard, C. and Cox, M. (1998) 'The criminality of former "special educational provision" permanently "excluded from school" adolescents as young adults (16–23): costs and practical implications', *Journal of Adolescence*, Vol. 21, pp. 609–20

Ram, M. (1992) 'Coping with racism: Asian employers in the inner city', *Employment and Society*, Vol. 6, No. 4, December, pp. 601–18

Rampton, A. (1981) *West Indian Children in Our Schools*, Cmnd 8273. London: HMSO

Ramsay, M. and Spiller, J. (1997) *Drug Misuse Declared in 1996: Latest Results from the British Crime Survey*, Home Office Research Study 172. London: Home Office

Rashid, H. and Rashid, S. (2000) 'Similarities and differences: working respectfully with the Bangladeshi community', in A. Lau (ed.) *South Asian Children and Adolescents in Britain*. London: Whurr Publishers

Raynor, L. (1970) *Adoption of Non-white Children: The Experiences of a British Adoption Project*. London: Allen and Unwin

Rees, G. (1993) *Hidden Truths: Young People's Experiences of Running Away*. London: The Children's Society

Rex, J. and Tomlinson, S. (1979) *Colonial Immigrants in a British Society: A Class Analysis*. London: Routledge and Kegan Paul

Rhodes, P. (1992) *Racial Matching in Fostering*. Aldershot: Avebury

Richards, A. and Ince, L. (2000) *Overcoming the Obstacles, Looked After Services for Black and Minority Ethnic Children and their Families*. London: Family Rights Group

Robinson, L. (1995) *Psychology for Social Workers, Black Perspectives*. London: Routledge

Robinson, L. (2000) 'Racial identity attitudes and self-esteem of black adolescents in residential care: an exploratory study', *British Journal of Social Work*, Vol. 30, pp. 3–24

Robinson, V. (1993) 'Ethnic minorities and the enduring geography of settlement', *Town and Country Planning*, March, pp. 53–6

Rowe, J. and Lambert, L. (1973) *Children Who Wait*. London: Association of British Adoption Agencies

Rowe, J., Cain, H., Hundleby, M. and Keane, A. (1984) *Long-term Foster Care*. London: Batsford

Rowe, J., Hundleby, M. and Garnett, L. (1989) *Child Care Now: A Survey of Placement Patterns*. London: BAAF

Rushton, A. and Minnis, H. (1997) 'Annotation: transracial family placements', *Journal of Child Psychology and Psychiatry*, Vol. 38, No. 2, pp. 157–9

Rushton, A. and Minnis, H. (2000) 'Research review: transracial placements – a commentary on a new adult outcome study', *Adoption and Fostering*, Vol. 24, No. 1, Spring, pp. 53–9

Rutherford, R. (1997) *Forever England: Reflections on Masculinity and Empire*. London: Lawrence and Wishart

Rutter, M. (1985) 'Resilience in the face of adversity', *British Journal of Psychiatry*, Vol. 147

Rutter, M., Maughan, S. and Smith, A. (1979) *15,000 Hours: Secondary Schools and Their Impact upon Children*. London: Open Books

Sammons, P. (1994) *Gender, Ethnic and Socioeconomic Differences in Attainment and Progress – A Longitudinal Analysis*. London: Curriculum Studies Department, Institute of Education

Scarman, The Rt Hon. Lord (1982) *The Scarman Report*. Harmondsworth: Penguin

Sellick, C. and Thoburn, J. (1996) *What Works in Placement?* Colchester: Barnardos

Sen, S. and Zaman, H. (1992) *'Just a Part of the Wall': A Report on the Services for Homeless Bangladeshi Women in Tower Hamlets*. London: Tower Hamlets Homeless Families Campaign

Sewell, T. (1997) *Black Masculinities and Schooling: How Black Boys Survive Modern Schooling*. Stoke-on-Trent: Trentham Books.

Shah, R. and Pattern, C. (2000) *Caring Alone – Young Carers in South Asian Communities*. Colchester: Barnardo's

Sharma, S., Hutnyk, J. and Sharma, A. (1996) *Dis-orienting Rhythms, The Politics of the New Asian Dance Music*. London: Zed Books

Shireman, J.F. and Johnson, P.R. (1986) 'A Longitudinal Study of Black Adoptions: Single Parent, Transracial and Traditional', *Social Work*, Vol. 31, 726–739

Simon, R.J. and Alstein, H. (1981) *Transracial Adoption: A Follow-up*. Lexington, MA: Lexington Books.

Simon, R.J. and Alstein, H. (1992) *Adoption, Race and Identity: From Infancy through Adolescence*. New York: Praeger

Sivanandan, A. (1978) 'From immigration control to induced repatriation', *Race and Class*, Vol. 20, No. 1

Small, J. (1984) 'The crisis in adoption', *International Journal of Psychiatry*, Vol. 30, Spring, pp. 129–42

Smetana, J. (2000) 'Middle class African American adolescents' and parents' conceptions of parental authority and parenting practices: a longitudinal investigation', *Child Development*, Vol. 71, No. 6, November/December, pp. 1672–86

Smith, D.J. (1977) *Racial Disadvantage in Britain*. Harmondsworth: Penguin

Smith, J. (1999) 'Youth homelessness in the UK, a European perspective', in *Habitat International*, Vol. 23, No. 1, pp. 63–77

Smith, P.M. and Berridge, D. (1993) *Ethnicity and Child Care Placements*. London: National Children's Bureau

Social Services Inspectorate (SSI) (1997) *For Children's Sake, Part 2: An Inspection of Local Authority Post-placement and Post-adoption Services*. London: Department of Health

Solomos, J. (1993) 'Constructions of black criminality: racialisation and criminalisation in perspective', in D. Cook and B. Hudson (eds) *Racism and Criminology*. London: Sage

Soni-Raleigh, V., Bulman, L. and Balarajan, R. (1990) 'Suicides among immigrants from the Indian subcontinent', *British Journal of Psychiatry*, Vol. 156, pp. 46–50

Stein, M. (1997) *What Works in Leaving Care*. Colchester: Barnardos

Stevenson, H.W. and Stewart, E.C. (1958) 'A developmental study of racial awareness in young children', *Child Development*, Vol. 29, pp. 399–409

Swann, Lord (1985) *Education for All: Final Report of the Committee of Inquiry into the Education of Children from Ethnic Minority Groups*, Cmnd 9453. London: HMSO

Taylor, J. (1976) 'Psychological development among black children and youth: a re-examination', *American Journal of Orthopsychiatry*, Vol. 46, pp. 4–19

Thoburn, J. and Rowe, J. (1991) 'Evaluating placements and survey findings and conclusions', in J. Fratter, J. Rowe, D. Sapford and J. Thoburn *Permanent Family Placements: A Decade of Experience*. London: BAAF

Thoburn, J., Norford, L. and Rashid, S. (1998) *Permanent Family Placement for Children of Minority Ethnic Origin*. Norwich: University of East Anglia.

Thomas, D.R. (1986) 'Culture and ethnicity: maintaining the distinction', *Australian Journal of Psychology*, Vol. 38, pp. 371–80

Tizard, B. (1977) *Adoption: A Second Chance*. London: Free Press

Tizard, B. (1995) 'Identity', in S. Jackson and S. Kilroe (eds) *Looking After Children, Good Parenting: Good Outcomes*. London: HMSO

Tizard, B. and Phoenix, A. (1989) 'Black identity and transracial adoption', *New Community*, Vol. 15, No. 3, April, pp. 427–38

Tizard, B. and Phoenix, P. (1993) *Black, White or Mixed-race*. London: Routledge

Tomlinson, S. (1987) Towards AD 2000: the political context of multicultural education', *New Community*, Vol. 14, pp. 96–104

Trivedi, C. (1997) 'Gang warfare', *Eastern Eye*, 2 May

Troyna, B. (1987) (ed.) *Racial Inequality in Education*. London: Tavistock

Tunstill, J. (1997) 'Implementing the family support clauses of the 1989 Children Act: legislative, professional and organisational obstacles', in N. Parton (ed.) *Child Protection and Family Support: Tensions, Contradictions and Possibilities*. London: Routledge

Turner, J.E. (1991) 'Migrants and their therapists: a trans-context approach', *Family Process*, Vol. 30, pp. 407–19

Ullah, P. (1987) 'Unemployed black youths in a northern city', in D. Fryer and P. Ullah (eds) *Unemployed People: Social and Psychological Perspectives*. Milton Keynes: Open University Press

Utting, W. (1998) *People Like Us, the Report of the Review of the Safeguards for Children Living Away from Home*. London: The Stationery Office

Vaughan, G.M. (1964) 'The development of ethnic attitudes in New Zealand school children', *Genetic Psychology Monographs*, Vol. 70, pp. 135–75

Virdee, G. (1992) *Issues of Ethnicity and Participation in Practice: Involving Families in Child Protection*. Norwich: University of East Anglia

Virdee, S. (1997) 'Racial harassment', in T. Modood *et al. Ethnic Minorities in Britain, Diversity and Disadvantage*. London: PSI

Wade, J., Biehal, N., Claydon, J. and Stein, M. (1998) *Going Missing, Young People Absent from Care*. London: Wiley

Waldinger, R., Adrich, H. and Ward, R. (1990) *Ethnic Entrepreneurs*. London: Sage

Walker, M. (1989) 'The court disposals and remand of white, Afro-Caribbean and Asian men', *British Journal of Criminology*, Vol. 29, No. 4, pp. 353–67

Ward, L. (2000) 'New Deal "less likely" to benefit ethnic minority youths', *The Guardian*, 11 February

Ward, R. and Jenkins, R. (eds) (1984) *Ethnic Communities in Business*. Cambridge: Cambridge University Press

Warheit, G.J. *et al.* (1985) 'Mexican-American immigration and mental health: a comparative analysis of psychological distress and dysfunction, in W.A. Vega and M.R. Miranda (eds) *Stress and Hispanic Mental Health*. Rockville, MD: National Institute of Mental Health

Waterhouse, S. (1997) *The Organisation of Fostering Services: A Study of the Arrangements for Delivery of Fostering Services in England*. London: NFCA

Whitehouse, P. (1983) 'Race, bias and social inquiry reports', *Probation Journal*, Vol. 30, pp. 43–9

Wilkinson, S.H.P. (1985) *Birth is More than Once: The Inner World of Adopted Korean Children*. Detroit: Harlow Press.

Woodward, W. (2001) 'Black community "needs own schools"', *The Guardian*, 20 June

Woolas, P. (2001) 'Beating the BNP', *The Guardian*, 15 June

Wrench, J. and Solomos, J. (eds) (1993) *Racism and Migration in Western Europe*. Oxford/Providence: Berg

Wright, C. (1987) 'The relations between teachers and African Caribbean pupils: observing multiracial classrooms', in G. Weiner and M.Arnot (eds) *Gender under Scrutiny: New Enquiries in Education*. London: Open University/Unwin Hyman

Youth Cohort Study (1998) Cohort 9, Sweep 1, Spring

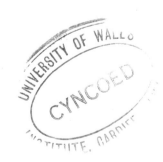